THE SINGLE-HANDED SAILING BUSINESS

Capt. Lyman Stuart

ISBN-13: 9798705388271

Cover design by: https://www.fiverr.com/ultrakhan22
Printed in the United States of America

CONTENTS

PREFACE

This book idea came from a phone call I received from a person on Long Island, NY. They asked, "How did you start your business?". For days after that initial call, I started thinking about how did I start. How was I able to keep it going for so long. According to data from the U.S. Bureau of Labor Statistics, "about 20% of U.S. small businesses fail within the first year. By the end of their fifth year, roughly 50% have faltered." Given that I have been able to keep this business going for over ten years, I felt it would be a good idea to share my approach and learning for others.

I have divided the book into three parts. Part 1 covers the time before opening my business and includes much of the work necessary to start a business. It consists of my thought process, which led me to a sailing business that I ran by myself. Part 2 covers the running of the company and the discoveries I encountered along the way, and finally, Part 3 includes the process of closing the business. The closing was a difficult decision, but I felt it was time to put it to rest and allow me to take a new direction in my life.

There are places in the text body that has a footnote. The text body talks in general terms and I placed a footnote referencing the specific solution that I used for the business. I leave the reason for a particular solution to the reader. A list of expanded footnotes can be found at the end of the book. Where it makes sense, I expand the general topic on why I chose it. I genuinely hope you will find this book informative and engaging as I take you on my journey to fulfill a dream.

PART 1

"I took a refresher class and Lyman listened to my needs and tailored his instruction to get the most of my time. He was very patient with me and knowledgeable. I will definitely continue learning under him in the future."

Chris H. 2018

1 IS THIS EVEN POSSIBLE?

I am sure ideas for starting a business come to people in many forms and at various stages in their life. For me, it came while taking my third certification at a sailing school here in Maine.

I started sailing at the age of twelve when my father sent me off to sailing camp. After that, I became his crew on his boat when he raced. Those summers through my teen years were memorable and exciting.

Life goes on, and I did not have much opportunity to do much sailing. Careers and raising a family took top priority. Once the kids were grown, my wife and I could fulfill our lifelong dream, buying a cottage on a lake. Now sailing could again be part of my life. After four years at the cottage, we realized that lake living was for us, and we wanted it to be year-round. With that, we bought a year-round home on another lake: a new lake, a bigger sailboat.

After a few lake sailing seasons, I started to wonder if ocean sailing would be my next step. That would mean a larger sailboat and, most likely, some formal training. The proper training, along with the certifications, was completed through two separate schools[1]. Each school had a unique perspective on learning style and location. One school conducted its lessons on a lake while the other was on the ocean. I found value in watching the owners of the two sailing schools conduct their business. It was also interesting to see two different learning styles. During the second ocean sailing course, starting my own sailing business came to me as a spark or flicker. It was strange that these flickers of an idea would pop into my head at the oddest times. Not quite enough to develop into a flame of a real plan. It was like someone or something was poking at me. "Is this even possible?" I would ask myself.

The business idea was starting to raise lots of questions. What should I offer, and how will I finance it? What should I charge? The biggest problem is where should I start.

Sailing lessons made sense to me since I enjoy teaching. Charters would be for those who did not want to learn but just wanted to get on the water and experience the joy of sailing. Since I was now planning to offer sailing lessons and charters, it made sense to show my capabilities. To accomplish that, I decided to seek a sailing instructor certification through the same parent company that gave me my regular sailing certifications. Winter in Maine is not a place to get certified as a sailing instructor, so I went to Florida for a week. There I completed two instructor certifications—one in basic keelboat and the other in coastal cruising. Having the instructor certifications would help with marketing.

Now that the certifications are complete, it was time to upgrade my current sailboat, which would suit the ocean. With the sailing business in the back of my mind, I wanted to find a sailboat large enough that people would feel safe aboard and yet not too large to overwhelm them. After a month of searching, I found a thirty foot Pearson with the right amount of amenities and features. The boat even came with a mooring at the boatyard that was selling it. I also had a marine survey completed for the vessel to alieve any concerns I may have had on its seaworthiness.

While my mind was still in the frame of wondering if this business idea is possible, it was time to do some research. I wanted to find out what my competition would be and if there would be a market for what I wanted to offer. I did online searches for local sailing businesses. I visited each one to see what they were offering and what their price structure entailed. I wanted to get a sense of how these businesses viewed their market. I looked at their bookings to see if they were overbooked or underbooked. That gave me a feel for demand. Overbooked would indicate a need and more potential customers. Expanding my search to other states yielded more insight into the marketing of a sailing business. The different prices were as wide as the Grand Canyon. It takes quite a bit of thought to develop a pricing structure that seems fair for the local market and yet high enough to cover expenses and hopefully draw a profit. Isn't that why you open a business anyway? The research resulted in a good feeling that another sailing business in the area would fit. So now what?

With questions still swirling in my head, I needed something that would prompt me to come up with the right answers. I was sure that I did not know what I did not know. Would there be something that would also raise the questions that I could or did not consider? I needed a business plan. So the first question is, do I write my own or draw from a template? Searching for a template took some patience and perseverance as there were far too many internet choices. I wanted a template that would organize my thoughts in a simple structure. One where I could fill in the blanks and make it mine. It needed to be suited to a single owner business.

Some were free, and some were purchasable. After days, yes I meant days, I found what I was looking for and spent the money to buy the template[2]. In the end, the price was well worth the effort and cost. Many of the sections had prefilled templated text, especially in the executive summary. The body text covered the sailing industry and highlighted the national trends for that industry. The template helped guide me through my objectives and mission statement, and therefore it gave me a purpose for the business. The section for start-up expenses offered a long list of what to consider. There were more items than I needed, but the ones I kept were a big help. Each entity then gave me something to consider. There was a services section that forced me to think about what I was offering to the public. I was able to add my research to the market analysis summary, which already had some templated text in the body. The market segmentation section focused on the type of customers I would go after—my actual target market. I was able to add the list of my direct competitors to the competitor's section, which I discovered from the earlier research. The strategy and implementation section focused on marketing and how my customers would find me. Again the template came with a lot of canned text suitable for the sailing industry. It was easy to embed some of my marketing thoughts within the existing text. I was able to remove those paragraphs that did not apply to my specific business. At the end of the business plan, there was a section titled competitive edge. The competitive advantage section took some thought but forced me to consider what will make my business different. One advantage that stood out above the rest was to offer all private sessions, so once someone booked an event, it would be just them and no others.

With the business plan complete and my questions uncovered and answered, it was now time to get serious. It appears that my flicker of a business idea has turned into a flame.

2 THE LICENSE

I cannot imagine a more bizarre time in my life where I have a full-time job in a career that has spanned some thirty-three plus years, yet I see a new direction for, eventually, another job. Am I ready to give up my day job? Not quite as I am a little too far away from retirement.

Seeing what is ahead of me to open my own business is like looking at a track field with many hurdles. Each hurdle is a task that will need accomplishing before the company can open. Most of these hurdles are independent of the others, but one stands out above the rest and is my first task. That task is the U.S. Coast Guard Captain's license.

Since I will be offering my services on Coast Guard controlled waters, I will need a captain's license. The Coast Guard has several captain's licenses, but given the size of my boat and what I want to offer my customers, it made sense to go for the Operator of Un-inspected Passenger Vessel (OUPV) or "six-pack" license. Without this license, I could go no further in opening a sailing business.

There are several items for the license application process, but the most time consuming is the small vessel sea service times[3]. One form for each vessel you report with months, years, and days when you were on the water. The total number of days needed is three hundred sixty in your lifetime; moreover, ninety of those days within three years of taking the exam. I figured I could use my Navy time, but I did not have any sea time records. To get those records, I sent a request to my U.S. Senator to see if she could retrieve them. It took a while, but she contacted the De-partment of Defense, and sure enough, my records came in a large package a few weeks later. Now I had to decipher the various military forms and pull out the dates and times that I was at sea during my three-plus years on the ship. A note on military service times, the Coast Guard only partially considers your sea time while in the service. I did not discover this little fact until after I initially submitted my application.

I was one hundred four days short of lifetime sea time. Fortunately, I had two boats at the lake house, one sail, and one power, which I recorded the days on the water in each of their forms. If you own a boat and are recording sea times, you will need to show proof of ownership for the Coast Guard to accept it. Using the new sailboat, I recorded over one hundred days on the water within the three years before the exam. Maine has an abridged boating season. During that time, I acquired ten people who wanted to go sailing, and therefore, I was able to offer them a chance to do just that. They became my crew whenever I was going to take the boat out. It was a perfect fit. I got to meet some new people, and they got the advantage of experiencing sailing. Some went on to purchase a sailboat of their very own. I located these people at a crew match party held each year at the boatyard, where I kept my sailboat. The crew match party puts boat owners with people who would like to crew. As I said earlier, this portion took almost three years to complete.

A section in the application requires proof of citizenship, so I included my birth certificate, social security card, V.A. file number, passport, and Transportation Worker Identification Card (TWIC) for the citizenship portion. The TWIC card required me to fill out the online application and then schedule an appointment at the local TSA office. The card's cost was $100, and the visit included fingerprinting, photo, and reviewing my proof of citizenship. The Coast Guard uses this program for their background check.

The application requires proof of a recent CPR and First Aid courses; three reference letters; however, I included copies of my sailing instructor certificates as well. A physical exam and drug test were the final documents needing completion and submission. These required scheduled appointments. The medical exam is within six months of the exam and the drug test within a year. I would suggest that anyone going through this effort is to get a checklist of requirements for the application process and ensure that it is complete before submitting it to the regional USCG office. All documents submitted must be original copies as the Coast Guard will make copies at the regional exam center and stamp them. Even though it was a two-hour drive, it was worth the trip to hand-deliver the documents. If possible, I would suggest you do the same.

Now I wait. Until the application is approved, I could not take the test. The USCG has a great site to show you the status of the application. The status site and associated credential state flow diagram alone saved much of the wonder of where my application was in the flow. I checked this regularly. Within a few short weeks, the approved application told me that I could now take the exam.

The Coast Guard license exam consists of five parts, Navigation, Plotting, Deck, Safety, and Rules of the Road, with questions drawn from over one thousand items. For the Rules of the Road portion, you must get a ninety percent or better.

So how would I study for such a test? Where would I get the material needed to feel confident in knowing the answers to the many questions? While researching a solution to help with this effort, I located a small software program that sat on top of a thousand-plus questions database. The interface was simple, randomized the items, and even allowed for filtering the questions to one of the five topics. I spent days using this program trying to get the right answer without looking at the answer given. Tried as I might, it was not enough to gain my confidence. I needed a new strategy and more research.

With a little luck and some creative Google searches, I discovered maritime training centers around the country that offer courses for those working toward a USCG Captain's license. They also provide the written exams right there at the training center, and the U.S. Coast Guard approves the tests. I choose Fort Lauderdale[4], which offered an eight-day immersion in all facets of what the exam expects.

The training center was great, and so were all of the instructors. Every night, the homework assignment consisted of copying a diagram of all of the navigation rules on a single 8 1/2 sheet of paper from a sample drawn by one of the former students. This exercise aimed to memorize this diagram became reference material during the "Rules of the Road" portion of the exam. Since you are given blank sheets of paper for your personal use during the test, the first task is to recreate that diagram I spent each evening copying[5]. I still have this laminated diagram today. I am amazed at how a single sheet of paper represents a book of one hundred ninety-eight pages.

Although the training was intense, I was able to find time to attend and acquire a couple of endorsements. One endorsement was the FCC license, while another was an "Auxiliary Sailing" endorsement. Each enhanced my license once I passed the exam.

The exams happen at the end of the session, one for each section. The navigation exam, even though only ten questions, took an hour and a half to complete. On one problem, I plotted all four answers and chose the one that was the closest.

To my delight, I passed all of the exams, and even though the training was intense, I could not have completed this task without it. So much of the material covered items I had never experienced, and the practice was invaluable.

Flying home, I realized that this idea of a sailing business just became closer to reality. The most challenging task was complete, and what started as a hurdle turned out to be a high jump—still accomplished but much more of a challenge than I initially expected.

3 MAKING IT LEGAL

It is now Fall, and I plan to open the business in the coming Spring. Lots to do to get ready for opening day. Again, so many questions like what will I use for a name, what type of business will it be, how much will my upfront costs be?

To start with, I needed to know what type of business should this venture be. Undoubtedly not a corporation as there is just me with no employees or staff. A sole proprietorship would be very easy to set up since you file a "Doing Business As (DBA)" and you are good to go; however, it offers no liability protection. A limited liability company (LLC) would make a better fit. It separates the business from my family and therefore shelters my family from any liability. Since it will be just me as the sole proprietor, I can file a single-member LLC; that way, I am taxed like a sole proprietor. As for the name, it must be unique. I decided to go simple and use my new titled name appended with "LLC." The result became Capt. Lyman Stuart, LLC. In Maine, I needed to submit the "Articles of Organization" and include a Limited Liability Agreement. The state of Maine supplies the first form as a fillable PDF file. I was able to locate a template for the second form and fill in what was necessary to define my business's legal aspects. The template already had much of the canned wording, which made life so much easier, and I then just needed to make it unique to my LLC. The filing cost was minimal, and within ten days, I received my approved request and DCN number. I did locate a website called "LLC University," which made this process more manageable and tailored for each state. I would encourage anyone going through this to check it out as it will save countless hours of frustration. To keep the LLC active, I will have to file an annual report with Maine; however, the state provides a simple online form with reminders sent out each January.

The next task is applying for an Employer Identification Number (EIN) issued by the IRS. The EIN will help separate the business from my Social Security Number and allow all money-related activities held in a designated bank account. Again, the point here is to keep the business separate from my personal assets.

With my new legal business name and a valid EIN, I went to the bank to set up the business checking account. I preloaded five thousand dollars into the bank account to cover what I imagined would be my upfront costs to get the business open. This value came from the business plan. Ordering checks got me to think of these little slips of paper as an opportunity for marketing, so I went with a nautical theme to go along with the checks' business name.

Now that I have a business checking account, I needed software to manage the information going through that account. The software must automatically download the bank's data, categorize the Schedule C entries, product business reports such a profit/loss and Schedule C. The software would then become my accountant. The one that I located did all of this and more[6]. I also created a three-ring binder divided into months. The binder will then contain all receipts and invoices in preparation for year-end tax purposes. Having the invoices and receipts broken down by months makes it easier to find the source of an uncategorized entry in the accounting software. A single envelope holds the small slip style receipts. A single manila envelope will then include all of the paperwork from the binder and marked with the year during tax time. Another benefit of the month tabbed binder is that I can put reminders on the tabs such a boat and mooring registration renewals, state annual LLC filing, insurance renewals, and membership reminders.

Insurance is the final legal entity, and this task is to locate commercial insurance for the business. As my sailboat is considered old in many insurance companies' eyes, it took a while to find one that would offer my business watercraft coverage. The insurance company is always evaluating the risk of the boat where customers will be on board. Offering a recent marine survey and showing my sailing certificates and experience helped with that effort. Soon I was able to locate a local insurance agent that offered what I needed. As I provided sailing lessons on the boat, I needed to have the insurance include a boat school usage endorsement. Also, since I was operating out a boatyard, I needed to have the boatyard copied on the insurance as another certificate holder, protecting the boatyard from liability. The insurance policy is another example of separating the business from my personal affairs. I went through another insurance company to define personal liability coverage when I was on another person's sailboat. One of the services that I would offer is to teach sailing on a customer's boat, helping them feel confident sailing their boat. This type of coverage is invaluable for preventing a customer from claiming that my lesson(s) was inadequate and causing an incident when the customer was sailing without me. Another insurance policy I acquired was haul-out insurance. This insurance would cover the costs of up to two thousand dollars to have the boat hauled out in advance of a storm for safekeeping while the storm came through the area. The policy I found cost only two hundred a year, and I feel it was well worth the expense to prevent the unexpected expense[7].

Regarding permits, licenses, and sales tax, Maine's state did not require any from these three categories for the services I offer other than the U.S. Coast Guard captain's license.

The last item on my list is to get permission from the boatyard to run my business there. I don't need a physical space in the boatyard, such as a storefront since my boat is where my customers will come to, but I did need to make the boatyard aware that I will be having customers come to me through their business. As I am a member and my boat is moored there, we worked out an additional business fee for my customers (nonmembers) to come to me. I also asked permission to use the boatyard's conference room, if available, to conduct one of the training classes. They agreed, and I worked up a legal agreement that we both would sign. The contract detailed the sailing school as a standalone business operating out of their location, offering both lessons and charters. I also requested that the boatyard guarantee me exclusive rights to run a sailing school out of this location. I listed the business name and that all on the water lessons and charters will be conducted by myself on my vessel, the Marisa III. My customers will pay the parking fee set by the boatyard.

I described my commercial insurance in the contract's insurance section, stating that it will be maintained by myself and cover the students and customers while on my vessel. The certificate holder of the policy will be the boatyard. My commercial insurance would cover me when I teach sailing on a boat other than the Marisa III.

In the contract's finance section, I agreed to pay the additional business fee; that I will accept checks, cash, or credit card, and all checks made out to Capt. Lyman Stuart, LLC; and if the boatyard receives any checks by mail, someone should forward them to me. In the final section of the contract, I asked for any calls or forms to the boatyard regarding my business that someone sends them to me. I gave them a thirty-day review period, and if all were to their approval, they sign their portion of the contract. I would encourage anyone who plans to run a sailing business out of a marina or boatyard, get permission first and make it a binding agreement so that each party knows the established boundaries. Nolo Press is a good source for templates like this[8].

The amount of legal paperwork was starting to gather at this point, so I created another three-ring binder to keep everything organized. I added dividers where each divider was a letter, so all things legal went into L; finance and bank account information went into F; insurance went into I. Business-related material such as the business plan and the start-up checklist went into B. I added a page at the beginning listing the letters and what went into each one as a quick reference and reminder.

4 GETTING ORGANIZED

The months have flown by, and it's now February, only three months until opening day. Getting organized is the process of structure creation, and the location of items is vital here. There is nothing more frustrating than knowing you have a document somewhere on the computer and cannot locate it. I don't particularly appreciate using the search feature. I am much more likely to anticipate where I can find an item, and when I see the document where I expected, I am quite happy.

Where to place electronic documents is my next challenge. I want to store the documents in a place that makes sense, is automatically backed up, and available on multiple devices such as my smartphone[9]. I realize that the folder structure will evolve throughout running the business, but I initially created it to support its initial needs. The highest level folder is the business name, followed by several subfolders. The insurance folder will contain all insurance items, such as the electronic version of the policies. Other folders are legal, lessons, forms, reference material, marketing, reports, and one for boat-related material named "Marisa III." As you contemplate your specific folder structure, consider how best to find any particular document. Don't make a mistake by lumping all information into a single folder.

As you create the various documents, consider the format, and ensure that you can view them via your smartphone. I cannot tell you how many times I have been on the boat and was thankful a document was available to me remotely. Having access to the remote reference material made it easy to email a copy to a customer while discussing it.

Since business emails will come through my only email address, I defined some rules to tag business-related correspondence. The rules evolved as emails came through. I also constructed a business signature to use when I replied to a customer. The signature included my title, name, phone number, and website address.

One of my customers' goals is to make it easy for them to see my availability. I have seen far too many sites that make seeing available dates and times too painful for the effort. It is one of the primary questions that any customer will be seeking an answer to when visiting a website that offers what I plan to offer. It took a while to find a free online availability calendar that showed what I needed for the sailing business. I only needed to show when I was available or booked. The one I went with had the added feature of showing when I was closed. Having the option of closed required updating the color and label of "Reserved." Each spring, I set up the year, marking the majority of days as closed, with the remaining days left as the available default. There were two ways to perform this task. One way was viewing the entire year with months as rows and days as columns. I then could select the day type of "Closed" and click each day that it applied. The second way was to choose the start date and end date, followed by the kind of day I wanted to show in the range. The second method was less time-consuming. The calendar displayed an annual calendar to the customer three months across the top and four rows down. As bookings came in, I signed into the calendar site and updated the specific date as booked. In each case, it required I do this task via the internet once I got home.

Since we are talking calendars, the Google Calendar has become my source for my bookings and serves as a critical reference. I would generally enter the start and end time of an event, along with the type of event and customer's name. A registration card will hold more detailed information on the booking. Adding a reminder and the sharing of the calendar with my wife is also helpful. Several bookings can happen on any given day, so this helps keep my wife abreast of my commitments. She can also edit the calendar for events that need my time. In such cases, I would then update the availability calendar as either "booked" or closed. Communication is key.

As I do not have a storefront or other physical location, there was no need for another phone line other than my cell phone. I did define a voice message greeting indicating to the caller that they reached my business when I could not take their call. The greeting was active between April and October. After that, I reverted it to my non-business greeting. Because I use my cell number as my business number, it does come with some risks. Since I cannot tell if an unknown number is a potential customer or a robocall, I needed to answer the call.

In looking for a service that can process credit cards, I needed one that did not require a customer to create an account or any login, for that matter. The refund process had to be simple and available through the internet. The one I ended up using allowed me to define each event type for each open day. The customer could then select the event and day and follow the payment options. I would get an email alerting me to the purchase. To get this to work, I defined all of the events for the entire season for charters and lessons. Fortunately, I was allowed to specify multiple days in one process, repeating this process for each event type. As one event became purchased, the others were marked as sold out, a manual task. I felt this was not the best solution but met the need for now. I would continue to look for an alternative.

I went with TripAdvisor for my customer reviews as I have used that service many times with great success. I view it as another form of marketing. Creating an account was easy and straight forward. I just needed to describe the business, add the phone number, email address, and eventually link it to a website. By adding the physical address, TripAdvisor will rank my company based on customer reviews. TripAdvisor has a feature called Review Express, which allows me to define any number of review requests that I can send out by supplying an email address(s). I constructed one template when I am on another person's boat and the second template when the customer is on my boat. The default when submitting a review request is to send a followup. I always deselected that option as I do not want to be pushy. One submission per customer is all that is needed. I also waited a few days before I sent the emails. Many of the customers are on vacation, so I want to wait until they get home.

5 THE WEBSITE

I view a website as central to my marketing presence, where all other efforts will point. In this era of searching for answers through the internet, visitors need to find you for any such marketing to become successful. Few customers will come if I don't exist, and you don't if an internet search places your website deep in the search results. I don't know about you, but I will rarely go beyond the fifth page of results. The challenge is to get near the top of any internet search but not in the ad space. Yes, you can pay for your site to appear with an "Ad" indicator and placed in the top results, but really, don't you visually scroll past the ads and get to the non-ad content? I know I do. How many search engines do you want to subscribe to for the advertisement services? If you do partake in this strategy, you will be paying for the clicks without knowing if the clicker will turn out to be a customer. As a small business owner with minimal marketing funds, I choose to skip this expense and spend my marketing budget elsewhere. My goal here is to develop a website that will find its way to the first page and when clicked, will engage the visitor to stay and explore.

There are several ways to develop a website and lots of services that offer a simple development environment. I have an advantage as my day job is in web-based development and interface design. I chose to have complete control of my website's design and construction[10] without being limited by the service that offers a development environment. I have acquired a few design rules over the years, which all come down to a single phrase for any visitor; "Don't make me think." As the website will only need basic HTML and CSS for its content, I can find a basic plumbing template to get me started. The template needs to be "responsive" to various screen types; computer, tablet, and smartphone. From there, I will tailor it to my specific needs. There is no need to start from scratch. I plan to publish the site in April, which gives me a little over a month to design and release it to the world. The website will become the initial marketing campaign before opening day.

I start with a list of customer questions. People arrive on a website looking for an answer to a question. Make sure you answer their question in a maximum of two clicks and no more than one page-down. The page-down guideline is ideal but not absolute. If you must have a long page, then order the most important to the least important content. For my sailing business, I envision the following customer questions which will need answering. What do you offer; what does it cost; are you available; where are you located; how can I contact you? Knowing these questions in advance will help with the design of the website.

People tend to scan a webpage top to bottom and left to right with their eyes. A good design test is to visit a random website, and once it is displayed, close your eyes and think of what you saw. Do you know what its purpose is? Does it engage you enough to explore more? A good study in what not to do for website design, although a little old, is to visit websitesthatsuck.com. Yes, that is a real website. It offers useful design considerations that still apply today.

A particular design has become popular in the past few years, and that being a single web page that scrolls through several sections. I find these designs frustrating because I don't particularly appreciate scrolling through useless content to get to what I want. Even if a search produces a link to the site, clicking the link provided just takes me to the top of the page. I believe that each page has a purpose and should dedicate itself to answer specific questions. I want to draw the visitor into the site, so a basic structure is in order. The top-level or home page will be the overview, answering the question about the offering. There will be two secondary pages; lessons and charters. These will appear as menu choices at the top of all pages. Click once, and the visitor will have the answers to offering details, price, payment types, and duration. Another click will show my availability within the second page through the calendar developed in a Google Sheet[11]. I will also offer the ability to prepay for the event via my online marketplace. Having separate pages for lessons and charters allows me to define unique descriptions and keywords for internet searching. This approach can also produce multiple lines in the search results. As mentioned before, my ten-second rule applies here; the user has ten seconds to know where to go next to answer their question.

Although not the original, discussed later, I will conduct a usability study with the completed website. During the usability study, I give a few people a task to perform on the website and see their effort to complete the job. I like to have my usability folks be of various ages, young and old alike. It's fascinating how different people perform the same task. Turning the initial questions into functions is an excellent place to start.

Additional pages for the website will include a contact page, a photo gallery, directions, and frequently asked questions (FAQ). The last item is a great place to place answers to prevent several customers from asking the same thing. The FAQ page will evolve as I cannot guess what people will ask. Some of these include, "Can you recommend a place to stay?" "Is there parking?" "What should I bring?". When I get the same question more than once, I consider its value for the FAQ page.

Crafting a website is like creating a sculpture out of clay; first comes the large portions followed by the details until your vision is there before you. I located a template and then spent quite a bit of time becoming familiar with the features it offered and how I could utilize them. Templates come with a lot of sample content, all of which needed to be removed and replaced with my website's content. Using the primary page layout from the template, I created the home page. The top will consist of a self-designed logo and a menu taking the user to the secondary pages. This menu will appear the same throughout the website, which will show consistency for the user. Below the menu will be a visual slideshow of ten or so pictures taken during the first two years before obtaining my captain's license. As I take more photos with some of the soon to meet customers, the images will find their way to the slideshow keeping the website fresh from year to year. I then add a tagline: "Your Time, Your Schedule, Your Adventure." I want to impress upon the customer that these events are all private, and as long as I am available when they want to go out on the waters of Casco Bay, they can.

The next section of the home page will summarize who I am and what I am offering, each with a short paragraph long enough to entice the visitor to seek more information. There will be a "Learn More" button in the Lesson and Charter segments, which will match the same name's menu choice. Clicking the button will take the user to the associated secondary detail page, further describing the specific offering. It's always a good idea to offer the user several means to the same end. Since the users' eyes are in one particular segment, it makes logical sense to provide them with an easy means to go deeper into the information.

The testimonials section of the home page will display selected reviews by the customers one at a time. As one fades, another will appear; a nice feature of the template. These, too, will be changed as reviews come in through TripAdvisor.

Weather plays a big part in any sailing adventure, so it made sense to show a forecast section on the home page, showing several days to help customers choose a day that works for them. I like the forecasts that offer not just the winds but also the gusts. So I'll locate a widget that includes this as well.

The next section allows the visitor to see a small promotional video no more than one minute in length—a short collection of photos set to music[12]. It is just enough to draw the visitor into the site and visually see what could be possible for them.

The footer section consisting of an About description and necessary Contact information will appear at the bottom of every page. I want visitors to contact me in any format they feel comfortable using and make it easy to find out how. The footer will also contain a copyright year, and since I don't want to have to change it each year, I will add a bit of Javascript automatically reflecting the current year. One less item to remember each year[13].

The Lessons page will have the title: "Private Sailing Lessons." Below the header will contain a picture of a customer engaging in a lesson followed by the various lesson types. Each lesson type will have a brief description, prerequisites, cost, payment types allowed, duration, and links to the availability calendar and online marketplace for purchasing online. The Beginner Sailing and Coastal Cruising course will be the only lessons that offer a certificate showing that the customer has completed the course. The certificate is my specific certificate and does not represent a certificate from any other sailing organization.

Even though I am a certified sailing instructor with the American Sailing Association (ASA), I chose not to be an ASA school. The requirements did not match what I wanted to offer. I would not have a physical presence or storefront, which was one of the major requirements. I will be using the ASA textbook, which I feel is superior in helping students understand sailing basics. My on-the-water sessions will reinforce the reading.

The Adult Refresher course will offer customized training to anyone who wants to hone skills that the experienced sailor feels less confident performing or had not experienced at all. The Private Lessons by the hour will round out the offering with a two-hour minimum. These are for people who are unsure how much time they needed and are willing to pay by the hour.

The last section of this page will include my Lesson Policy. Here I will describe the registration process, the class schedule, what to bring, the cancellation policy, and refunds.

For the Charter page, the title is "Private Charters," followed by Day Sail and Evening Sail descriptions. Each type will include the definition, cost, duration and schedule, and links to the availability calendar and online marketplace to prepay the event.

The Contact page will have a Google map showing my location.

To offer this, I needed to create a Google business profile that was reasonably simple to accomplish as I already had the business email account through Google. Once completed, I just needed to embed a frame into the page, reflecting my business's physical address. There will be a simple form for the user to fill out, sending me a message in an email, requiring only their name, email address, and a brief message. I will include a ReCaptcha checkbox to protect my site from spammers and abuse. I will also have all the communication methods showing my email address, phone number, physical address, mailing address, and operations hours. Here I listed May-Oct 8 am to sunset.

To give the visitor a complete idea of what sailing on the Marisa III is like, I will create a Photos page that will contain a three-minute movie/slideshow complete with background music. The initial video will include preopening photos with family and friends. More recent images will replace older ones in the video to keep it fresh and current as time goes by.

Although the Contact page includes directions, I wanted to have a dedicated page for more information. Again, this will consist of the Google map showing my location and step-by-step directions from the North or South. I will also offer an aerial view of the boatyard with Google Earth's help, pointing out critical places, gatehouse, parking, dock store, on the premises. The aerial view will help those customers who are unfamiliar with the area and facility to find me.

One final page of the website will be the Frequently Asked Questions (FAQ). Here the template had a control that allowed for expanded text when someone clicks on a question. That will enable the initial presentation to be a list of items quickly scanned by the visitor. One-click, and they have the answer. For the initial version of this, I added a handful of questions that I envisioned the customer would ask. Over time, the list will grow, with the more common ones at the top of the list.

It took a few weeks to get the initial design complete and the content the way I wanted it—a few tweaks to the text, some replacement of items, and color scheme finalized. Using a local development environment made the work go much quicker than developing on the web-based service. Still, there is a limit to what can be done locally without placing it on the internet. It was time to publish the work to a hosting company.

Choosing a hosting company with the requirements I needed took some company comparisons. I also needed to develop a domain name for the business, one that was easy to say and one that would reflect my business. Looking at my business email address made this effort relatively straightforward, and therefore, gosailingcascobay.com was born. It is unique globally, similar to the business email, and is almost a complete sentence in itself. "Do you want to go sailing on casco bay?"

I needed an affordable hosting company that included the purchase and management of a domain name, 24/7 tech support, reliable uptime, and the ability to host my website through FTP (File Transfer Protocol). I will continue developing and testing locally and then publishing the changed content via FTP to the hosting company when I am satisfied with the change(s). The company I went with[14] also offered a free Secure Sockets Layer (SSL) certificate. Google requires the SSL to get the search result to appear near the top, and having one allows me to have the "HTTPS" prefix to the website address, ensuring security for the visitor from hackers. I would encourage anyone who publishes a website to do so with an SSL Certificate.

With the domain name in place and the initial website published to the hosting company, it was now time to tune the site for searching. The tuning process takes time and equates to the detail of a clay sculpture. The process is to add keywords, description, title text, optimize the page display speed, and ensure the header tags are search-friendly. Each page within the website should have its own focus drawing different users for different reasons. The Charter page is for visitors interested in going for a sail without a classroom setting structure. The Lesson page will be for visitors interested in learning how to sail. The keywords for each page will maximize the number of characters that are allowed. The page description also has a limit as this is what will appear below a search result. It should be descriptive enough to briefly explain the content and cause the visitor to explore more. I looked at keywords from other sailing charter companies and sailing schools to get a sense of what may work. I then added a few words and phrases that are specific to my business. Some examples are "Portland, Maine," "casco bay." It is good to think about what search words potential customers will be using. The more times a keyword appears within the website, the more likely the page will appear in the search results. Using a Search Engine Optimizer (SEO) tool is a great place to start[15]. These tools can give you keyword ideas based on your content, point out errors, and help get the site higher within the search results. That's the whole point. I spent days tuning the site for just the right combination of words and phrases until the results started to appear on the first page of Google search. The entire focus was to improve my ranking and not just Google but many of the other search engines.

The idea of ranking among search engines brings up the concept of website submission. The indexing of the website was necessary to improve the results of a search. To ease this burden, I needed to find a website submission tool that submitted the website to as many search engines as possible. Once found, I entered my website address and clicked Submit. Research showed that by adding meta tags, a Google-generated sitemap, and a ROR (Resources of a Resource) file, the search engines would better understand the content. After a week, I started to test various search phrases that I speculated would be used by potential customers looking particularly at which words were bolded in the brief descriptions of the results. I even used phrases and words from area competitors to see if I ranked higher than them. With some more tweaks and tuning, which included adding some meta tags and selective files to the website, my website started to appear closer to the first page of results.

I discovered that backlinks are another method for improving a site's ranking. To create backlinks, I needed to find (or make) places to reference my website. TripAdvisor was one place that I added a reference. In another instance, I signed up to become a member of the Maine Tourism Association. There I added a summary of my business with a link to my website. In searching for other sailing businesses, I discovered additional free service sites that allowed me to add my listing to their directory. The purpose here is to get as many external sites pointing to my website.

I tested the site with various devices and browsers involved asking my friends and family to visit the site and give me their impressions. There were online tools to view the website with different browsers and smartphone simulations. Some of the results caused some more tweaking and retest until I got the results I needed.

It is now April, and the website has been live for two weeks. It was now time to monitor the site traffic. The hosting company includes visitor statistics of the site by month. I can see how many visitors I had on any given day within the visitor stats, where geographically they were coming from, and what keywords (if any) they used to find the site. Using my Google account, I created a Google Analytics account. I then added Google Analytics to the home, lesson, and charter pages, which were the only pages I am interested in tracking. Through this service, I can track the site's speed, which referral sites send visitors to me, keywords used, geographical locations of the visitor down to the city level, type of device, and ability to watch a user currently live on the site. I particularly like the weekly comparison summary of visitors. Google Analytics even has a smartphone app version of the statistics, making it easy to view the results anywhere at any time.

After spending the last few weeks designing, tuning, and monitoring the now published website, it feels like I crafted a fishing lure and took it to a well-stocked stream only to find that both banks are full of other folks fishing for the same catch. Here is to hoping my lure works.

6 SUPPLIES

The website is now up and running smoothly; monitoring and adjusting will be an ongoing process. It's time to start gathering the supplies for the sailing business's daily operation. Opening day is only a few weeks away, and there is already interest from prospective customers.

Business cards would be an excellent place to start, although designing one might seem a bit daunting. Have you ever looked at the pegboard in a restaurant? And noticed all of those business cards, each trying to catch your eye? Take five or more business cards and place them on the floor at random. Stand back and look at them and see which one or two catches your eye. From the ones you have chosen, can you tell the type of business from a distance? Some are shiny; some are not; some have color, and some do not. Which ones appeal to you? For me, color was a must, and glossy was better than not. Some cards used one side while others used both. It makes sense to maximize the space available with minimal information. The ten-second rule applies here too. My business card will contain a sailboat image, my business name, contact information, where I am located (since that is different from my mailing address).

The top third will be a dark blue bar with white lettering for the business name and tag line. The bottom two-thirds will have black lettering for the additional information, including the website address, and that I am an ASA Certified Sailing Instructor. The sailboat image from a stock image library will appear on the left. On the back will be the text "Go Sailing" above a photo that I took of a sunset from the Marisa III deck, followed by the website address. The card will have a gloss finish, and the text will be in "Times New Roman" font except for "Go Sailing," which will be in a "Brush Script" font and matches the business logo on the website. Now where to find a reasonably priced service that allows me to design the card online. A quick Google search for "business cards" resulted in a great company just below the "Ad" results. The first one hundred for fifteen dollars seemed fair enough, but the service recommendation of five hundred was only twenty dollars. Well, five hundred seemed a bit excessive for starting, so I split the difference and went with two hundred fifty. The design center was seamless, intuitive, and fun. Going through the steps in the design environment took about an hour. Well worth the time spent. The preview feature was great, and ordering was a breeze. Oh, and shipping was free.

I noticed on the business card service that they offered "rack cards," too. If you have ever seen those information centers with tons of businesses in the racks, these are those types of cards. Something easy that people can take away and read later. I have seen people at these information centers grabbing several at a time, not reading them, just saving them to read later. Again the design is crucial and needs to catch the eye of the browser. Many racks show only the top half of the card, so the card's top will need eye-catching information.

The rack card designer was as easy as the business card designer[16]. I chose to have a full image background of a sailboat moored on the water at sunset, one that looked much like the Marisa III. The text at the top of the card will be "Go Sailing" in the same Brush Script font. The text below this will be a smaller font and read: "in the heart of Casco Bay." The result is a complete sentence and indicates both what and where. The card's bottom will summarize my offerings, my name, phone number, and website address. The back of the rack card will show a brief description of sailing lessons and private charters. The physical address, phone number, email address, and website address will appear at the bottom. I'll have a photo showing the boat's bow with an island in the background on a cloudless summer day. I'll include that as well. I also added a "QR code" to the lower portion of the card, which will take them to my website when scanned by a smartphone. I was able to generate the image online through a QR code generator. All I needed was to enter the web address.

As a member of the Maine Tourism Association, I can now place my rack cards in two visitor centers of my choice. A relatively straightforward decision as there are two along the Maine turnpike that is near where I live. A visit to each one involved introducing myself and my business so that the staff had a better understanding when tourists asked questions regarding sailing in the area. Marketing has begun. I left a stack of cards to place in their information stands, which even had a section devoted to sailing. There before my eyes, I saw some of my competition. I then took a few of their information to read later and compare. Chalk this one up to more research.

Now, what to wear? I am thinking of a casual, professional look. Polo shirt with simple abstract sailboat design, title and name, and the phrase "Go Sailing" placed over the left chest. No particular color, so maybe a variety; white, dark blue, and black. The same for a fleece when the weather is colder as found in May, June, and the Fall. I won't need that many of those, so that a single color will do. Designing these and ordering was accomplished through the same online service as the business cards. This company is now becoming my go-to shop, and through their suggestion, I ordered labels too.

Opening day is now just days away, and I have my first customer scheduled for June. Gathering customer information in the form of a registration card is next on my list of supplies[17]. I briefly thought of creating a database for customer information. Too technical for my liking, which is odd since my day job is in IT. I feel the same way with recipes. Yes, a database of recipes might be fun to search and scroll through; however, nothing beats pulling out a recipe card, laying it on the counter, and following along.

Nonetheless, I will instead design an actual card to touch and feel—contact details on the top of the card, including three types of phone numbers and an email address, followed by event information such as event type and date, enough entries for eight events. If a customer ends up with eight events, that event will be free—an unadvertised perk. The blank back of the card will contain more information regarding the customer. Here I can add family member names, personal interests, age, sailing experience, and other pertinent information to make the event more welcoming, mainly if they come back for another sail.

The cards will be four and one-quarter by five and one-half inches in size, so I can use the Avery 8387 postcard card stock for printing a sheet of four cards. Selecting this layout in the word processor makes the design easier as I can see where the boundaries are for each card. Designing one card in the first provided space, I then just copied and pasted it into the other three areas. I then saved the document as my registration card template. I would then print the number of sheets that I needed for the season.

For a start, I printed ten sheets yielding forty cards. These are pre-perforated so separating the individual cards is easy. Given my first customer, I entered their information on my first registration card. To store the cards, I found a wooden box that can handle the size. Pretty sure it was a wooden recipe box painted white with a flip-top that I found alone in an antique shop. It even came with some blank dividers. I named the tabs upcoming, gift certificates, current season, and blanks. The cards in the "upcoming" section will contain customer cards for future events ordered in date order. Once completed, the card will move to the "current season" section sorted alphabetically by last name, and any additional notes added. The "gift certificate" section will contain prepurchased events with no chosen date. The setting of the date will then cause these cards to move to "upcoming."

I believe that more information is better for a customer who may be new to the area or sailing. They may not know where to find me or what is expected of me while sailing on the Marisa III. A flier, or several types, is in order[18]. Each is to be limited to a single page, will answer many questions from a customer conversation, something they can use as a reference. For any event requested by a customer, I can attach the appropriate flier to the confirmation email. All of them will have the same necessary information about the "Marisa III," where they will be sailing from, what to expect, what to bring, parking details, a link to my website, my phone number, and email address. The top left will contain a photo of my sailboat. The lower right will include an image of my business card. If the customer had not prepaid for the requested event, then a link to the online marketplace will be available to them in the flier; otherwise, I will include a confirmation of their purchase.

I designed a flier with a gift certificate at the top for customers who purchased a gift certificate. In the word processor, I then add the details to the gift certificate, which includes "Presented To," "Item," describing the purchased event, From, Issue Date, and the Certificate Number. I created a general gift certificate and another one with a nautical winter scene for the holidays. I made a spreadsheet on the business' Google Drive to keep track of the gift certificates, including the purchaser's information. The remainder of the flier is an abridged flier to have the document fit on a single page. I then print it to PDF and attach it to the email.

The beginner sailing course's classroom portion will consist of ten slides, printed, placed double-sided, and laminated[19]. For the knot tying exercises, a self-made knot tying board made from my wife's old cutting board where I attached a five-inch cleat, a three-quarter-inch wooden dowel three inches long fixed vertically in the board, and a one and a half-inch eye hook. There will be three one-quarter-inch braided lines, five feet in length, to go with the board.

To help students understand the "rules of the road" when sailing, I constructed two wooden sailboats cut from three-quarter-inch pine blocks, three inches long and one inch wide. Each hull is teardrop shape painted white. At the bow, I placed a small red semicircle sticker on the port side and a green semicircle sticker on the starboard side. For the mast, I cut two quarter-inch dowels six inches in length. I used the same material as the mast for the boom but cut it to one and a half inches long. I created two eye hooks from copper wire to attach the boom to the mast, which allowed the boom to swing at the connection point. The final piece was the mainsail, which was nothing more than some cotton cloth I had and cut to a length that would allow me to hot-glue the fabric to the mast and the boom. I created a three-inch by three-inch arrow made from a thin veneer painted white, representing wind direction. In combination with the model sailboats, it can show the difference between a starboard tack and a port tack, upwind, and downwind[20]. Sometimes a visual representation is better than a textbook diagram. The student then gets to see the various combinations of wind to sailboat and boat to boat relationships related to the wind direction.

I ordered twenty ASA textbooks for each course for a starting supply from Amazon. I purchased parallel rulers, dividers, mechanical pencils, soft erasers from the local marine supply store and located a mock chart sample and associated problems for the coastal cruising course's classroom session. This course will be heavily focused on navigation with the first three hours in a classroom setting so that these tools will be necessary.

For the tests at the end of each course, I pulled together a list of multiple-choice questions from the U.S. Coast Guard exam database. The beginner course will consist of twenty-five questions, while the coastal cruising course will be thirty-two. I saved an instructor's copy with the answers in bold and indications where the student would have found the topic in their reading. If it were not in their reading, then it would be discussed and marked accordingly. Since each test is a multiple-choice test, I located a standard marking sheet to gather the answers. Once the student has completed the course, they will receive a custom-designed completion certificate using eight and one-half-inch by eleven-inch card stock.

I created a waiver form for all students to sign and bring to the first day of class.

Opening day is now very close, and I have my first students, a couple from Virginia, coming in May. I then put together the first student materials packet to be mailed, including the textbook, a rack card, the waiver form (one for each student), and a flier for beginner sailing. A note when mailing any book through the U.S. Postal Service, be sure to say that you are sending "media" mail. It will save you a lot of money.

Now I wait.

PART 2

"Great way to see Casco Bay. Can't wait until next spring for sailing lessons. Had a ton of fun sailing into Portland and being able to see the cruise ships and sailboat races. Highly recommend."

Josh 2015

7 A TYPICAL YEAR

Maine winters go on far too long, and I have heard that April in Maine is a winter month, so having a few warm and sunny days during that month is a blessing, even if there is still snow in the boatyard. Getting the boat ready for the season is a labor of love. I start by placing my sixteen-foot ladder to the deck and climb through the zippered door into the shrink wrap. It can be quite warm inside the shrink wrap if the sun is out, even if the temperature outside is fifty degrees. Armed with cleaning supplies, I begin cleaning the interior top to bottom, inspecting any mold areas that may have developed over the winter. If found, I spray them with mold and mildew remover and wipe them clean. I remove all items from the lockers and inspect each one for mold and then clean the space itself. I check for any evidence of critters that may have found their way in for their winter home. Fortunately, I have never seen any indications in the past years I have owned the boat. Batteries are brought onboard, placed in the starboard locker, and connected. Cabin lights checked.

I cut the shrink wrap just below the rub rail to expose the hull yet keep the boat covered. This technique allows me to clean and polish the hull above the waterline, sand, and paint below the waterline. Because the vessel resides in saltwater throughout the season, I use special ablative paint[21] to prevent marine growth from developing. Even though the paint is considered multi-season, I repaint the bottom every year in the color of a deep blue sky. Odd that it turns black when it is first put on yet takes on its final blue color by the time it is in the water. Every few years, I repaint the boot stripe, which is a bright red.

Within a week of its launch date, I prep the freshwater tank with a mixture of lemon juice and a water treatment solution[22]. Once I fill the tanks and lines, I let the mixture sit there for an hour to remove any bacteria and odors that have developed since its last use. After the hour, I drain the tank and lines, close the drain, add the correct amount of water treatment for the tank's size, and refill with fresh water. The water that I have onboard will make it through the entire season without filling or retreating. Given that the usage of water is for cleaning dishes and hands only, seventeen gallons is plenty. Not for drinking, for sure.

Removing the shrink warp amounts to cutting a line down the middle of the boat along the wooden frame's upper ridge. The plastic then just falls away from the deck to the ground. The bow and stern pulpits take extra effort as the plastic is gathered and heated to multiple layers. With only the frame remaining, I take the screw gun removing the many screws that keep the structure together. I am careful when dropping the wooden slats to the ground. I need to take care of my boat and the boats on either side that are only a few feet away. The uprights are two by three, and they, too, are carefully tossed over. There is a gathering area in the boatyard where all of the framing material is stacked for eventual reuse in the next season. The recyclable shrink wrap is gathered together and rolled up for the boatyard folks to pick up.

I now look at the compilation of boats in various readiness stages, all resting peacefully on their cradles, like infants waking from their long winter nap. The boatyard has taken on an air of activity with the boat owners working to ready their boats, all with a wish for a good boating season. As I stand on the now open deck, I can see out over Casco Bay with the sparkle on the water, islands in the distance. I am lost in a daydream, remembering the seasons past and the happiness I feel being on the boat, the sound of the sea flowing along the hull. The bay calls out, "Come play." "Soon. soon." I tell her.

OK. It's time to get back to work. The cleaning of the deck is the next task now that it is open to a sunny day. I run a hose to the deck from a nearby faucet, fill a bucket with boat soap[23] and grab the deck brush. Wetting it down with the hose followed by scrubbing with the brush dipped into the pail of soap. "Magic Eraser" and a spray of Simply Green makes those hard to clean areas a simple chore. A must to any boat cleaning supplies. The cushions are put back aboard along with the radar console, binoculars, and charts. I reattach the dodger to its frame, hang the anchor from the bow pulpit, and put the Lifesling system on the stern rail.

My work here is done, and it is now up to the boatyard to launch her for the season. A few weeks before, I filled out the commissioning form to request my launch date, usually a few days before the launch service starts for the season. On that form, I additionally request the commissioning of the engine and any other work I would like completed before opening day. I leave a booklet in the galley, a series of images with notes, for the riggers, which shows how to rig the Marisa III. The riggers have well over one hundred boats to put together, and they cannot know each boat's particulars. A few mistakes on my boat were the reason for developing the booklet in the first place. They have since said how much they appreciate the booklet. In the booklet, there are images and notes of the roller furler, boom vang, topping lift and outhaul, main sheet, and masthead. Every two years, I leave a new impeller on board for the engine commissioning. It is a small price to pay to ensure that a disintegrated impeller does not get into the heat exchanger.

In preparation for opening day, the boatyard gets the boat ready for the season by putting the mast back on the boat, rig her for the season, and place her on the mooring—one of the benefits of belonging to this boatyard. Mast lights checked, engine put back together and tested. Once on the mooring, I further ready the boat, which includes bending on the sails, jib sheets attached to the headsail, and run back to the cockpit. The deck is cleaned again, and stanchions are polished. The annual shakedown cruise is the first outing to ensure that the spring commissioning is complete. Through this, I check the VHF radio, radar, sails, lines, and engine; I bring aboard bottled water and ginger ale for the customers, or anything ginger, a good remedy for seasickness.

Each year, before the launch service begins for the season, I row out to the mooring and attach a ten-foot fiberglass rod to the mooring pennant using cinch ties. It took a few years to discover this trick to prevent the pennant from tightly wrapping around the mooring ball. Once this happens, it became near impossible to grab the pickup mooring stick when I returned from a day on the water. I am sure my customers found this amusing. I did not. When the winds were light, I could spend a fair amount of time on the bow unwrapping the line from the mooring ball. Not sure if the line had wrapped clockwise or counterclockwise. This would involve getting the boat hook and grabbing the wrapped line and unwinding it—much more challenging in higher winds. Early on, I tried adding "noodles" to keep the line floating on top of the water. A good idea in theory but failed in practical use. Having a pickup buoy was a blessing as it made getting back to the mooring easier single-handed.

The height of the stick needs to be high enough to see it from the cockpit. I idle the engine, put the gear in neutral, coast the boat straight to the stick. Once the stick is near the bow, I then head forward and grab the stick before getting to the second stanchion. No boat hook needed. I pull the stick aboard below the bow pulpit rail and then grab the mooring loop and place it on the bow cleat—home safe.

Regarding the pennant loop placement, I have seen people put the loop through the cleat and then spread it over the two ends. I have found that this method makes it difficult to cast off as the loop can get very tight on the cleat from the boat's constant tugging against the mooring. It also takes time to get this set while trying to keep the boat steady against a breeze. I prefer to place the loop around the cleat and then make the circle smaller with a series of clove hitches using a short line, always attached to the pennant loop and at the ready. Casting off amounts to just untieing the small line and remove the pennant from the chock. Throw everything overboard, including the pickup buoy—prepared for the return.

Opening day. Each year on this special day in May offers such possibilities. I have a handful of customers booked. Every year the staff at the boatyard will ask, "How does your season look?" of which I always say the same thing; "Ask me in October." The season of customers seems to be a two-week rolling wave. Booking weeks in advance is a rarity, not the norm. I am always amazed at how the calendar fills in, with July and August being the busiest months by far. After the season ends, the bookings look like a sine wave. Slowly rising from May through June and falling off from September to October.

Running the business through the season single-handedly, I play every role from the call center, booking agent, administrative assistant, instructor, charter captain, accountant, and heaven knows what else is in the mix. The typical booking will start with a phone call from a customer asking for more information. They may ask about availability or how they can pay in advance. With questions answered and we agree on a date and time, I will verbally say they are confirmed and send more information through email. On my smartphone, I immediately mark the date as booked on the Google Drive availability calendar to prevent double-booking. All of my offerings are private, so once someone secures a date, it is theirs and theirs alone. Once I get home, I will fill out the customer registration card[24], mark the event with "(pd)" if pre-paid, and add any notes that I heard from our conversation. I also send out a confirmation email and attach the appropriate flier and directions to the dock. The registration card is then placed into the registration box in the upcoming section in the proper location by date. I then add the event to the calendar that I share with my wife and set a reminder for the upcoming event.

I wait until the end of the sail for charters to ask the customer how they would like to pay. Paying after, especially by credit card, allows them to add a tip. It is less likely to happen if they pay in advance. Some customers are not familiar with tipping a charter captain, and when asked, I will always say, "It is not required but very much appreciated." I must say that having the ability to take a credit card while still on the boat is a huge benefit. The card reader's latest model even added contactless payments, on top of the regular swipe and chip reader capabilities. A student must pay for beginner and coastal cruising courses in advance and online. That gives me the information needed to mail out their course material. Yes, another job included in my single-handed business; mail clerk. I encouraged all students to book at least two weeks before the course starts to provide them with time to read the textbook. In the cases of pre-paid events, if for any reason the customer cannot make the event, I tell them they can either reschedule or receive a refund. If the customer wishes a refund, I will take on the billing clerk's role and issue the refund through the credit card processing service if paid online or a check if paid by check.

Regarding canceled events, I do have the option to keep the calendar marked as booked, which gives me a day to myself. In July and August, this is a rare and welcomed treat. A solo sail on a warm summer day is one way to relax and enjoy being out on my own. When the wind calls me, I rarely refuse.

On several occasions, my first notification that I have a customer is when my credit card service notifies me of a purchase. After this, the customer will call me or email me to seek additional information or set a date. If they don't, I will then give them a call to discuss their recent purchase. I much prefer one on one communication rather than having everything completed electronically through a booking service. It allows me to ask questions such as how many are in the group or the children's age. The latter is useful to know to ensure I have the proper life jackets when they arrive. I keep extra life jackets at the dock store for just such situations.

I handle all forms of communication with my customers, and it has only been in the last few years that text messaging became a familiar form. I am not surprised. There have been times when I receive a phone call while on the water. I can remember more than once when I asked the customer to hold for a second while taking the boat through a tack. When I get back on the call, the person on the other end will ask, "Are you on the water right now?" at which I reply, "Yes." I get the impression that they enjoyed being part of the experience and helped secure them as a customer. I try to return all communication by the end of the day or sooner whenever possible. I let phone calls go to voice mail if I am genuinely unavailable at the moment. I don't like to be left hanging, and I don't expect my customers to go through the waiting either. If they are waiting for my reply too long, they will go somewhere else. Other potential customers will use the contact form on the website to ask me questions. The resulting email allows me to get back to them with answers and suggest that they give me a call to discuss further in person. The more opportunities I have to talk with them in person, the better the chances are to confirm an event.

I have gotten pretty good at knowing who my customers are as they walk to the dock among the several families heading out for the day. They have this searching look and an expression of amazement when they first see the mooring field of sailboats bobbing on their mooring. I already know how many in the group and if there are kids. Knowing the age of the kids helps with this as well. For the students, they usually have their textbook with them. The first question after the introductions is usually, "Where's your boat?" I would then reply with "Out there." waving my arm across Marisa III's general location. With twelve hundred boats off the dock, it's just easier to be a little vague. With greetings completed, we head down the pier to the launch, which takes us out to the boat, including others heading out to their vessel. The customers did not expect such a service and found the short ride a pleasant addition to the day. They have a look of anticipation as the launch passes many of the other vessels. As we near a boat, do they wonder if this is the boat we will go on? Once we get close to the Marisa III, I'll say to them, "There she is." The launch pulls up along the starboard side, and I get on to the boat, helping my customers get aboard too.

I open up the cabin, grab any bags they have brought, and place them below. I give the customers the three cushions to be placed in the cockpit, open up the seacocks, turn on the electronics, grab winch covers, placing them below along with the tiller cover. At this point, for charters, I ask the customers if any have sailing experience. If not, I ask them if they want to help with crewing the boat. On yes, I give them a quick lesson on winch handling and controlling the jib sheets, emphasizing that they watch their fingers. A thrill comes over their face at the anticipation. I turn on the engine, cast off the mooring, and our day begins.

When we return, the usual question is, "How do we get back to the dock?" Sometimes I'll say, "Well, there is always swimming, but I prefer to call the launch on the radio, after which they come to pick us up." Back on the dock, we say our thank yous and good-byes, and the day ends with a few more memories created and smiles shared.

The remainder of the season frequently repeats similarly, with the only change being the people and the weather. In a way, it is nice to have a routine that can be relied upon and yet make each outing unique and special.

September brings the decommissioning request, where I put in the date for the boat to be hauled out and prepped for winter storage. I will add any additional work that I wish accomplished as part of this process. The haul-out date is usually the second week in October, soon after the season's launch service stops.

October brings the tallying of the season. Tallying involves going through all current season registration cards, counting the customers' location, and the event types. The master deck of cards will now include those cards by the customers' last name as I move one set to another. I take everything off the boat and bring them home for the winter. Once she is on the cradle and the engine is decommissioned, I take the batteries home too.

Although I regularly keep up with the accounting portion of my job throughout the sailing season, I do a final check in the accounting software to ensure that all transactions have Schedule C categories. A nice feature of the accounting software[25] is that it allows me to define any category label I wish and then associate it with the actual Schedule C category. Doing this makes sense for my business when I run a Profit/Loss or tax report and is easy to transfer to the spring's tax software[26].

November gets me into the holiday spirit and is when I offer the holiday gift certificates. The offer involves updating the website with the announcement and remains there until the day after Christmas.

The new year brings registrations both boat and mooring, setting up the availability calendar for the coming season, and Schedule C. I run a few other year-end reports to close out the prior year and file them in the reports folder for future comparison with previous years. I remove all of the binder's receipts and invoices, placing them all into a manila envelope, marking it with the year they represent and keep for seven years.

In February, I offer a preseason 10% discount for any customer that purchases an event online. I define the deal through the credit card service indicating the start and end dates, and then on the website, I post the announcement along with the discount code.

March is the filing of the annual taxes with the IRS. That's plenty for this month. I start thinking of the coming season and hope for warm weather to arrive earlier than before—wishful thinking on my part.

And now we are back to where we started—another year ahead with more possibilities.

8 CHANGE

Throughout the running of this business, I realized that change is inevitable. Be it from outside forces or my wish to make a change for the better. I have heard that "Change is good." For who or what? Dealing with change is the real challenge; however, being flexible helps to lessen the burden. As Jimmy Dean once said, "I can't change the direction of the wind, but I can adjust my sails to always reach my destination."

The website went through the most change to the business consisting of three separate versions with minor modifications within versions. Some of these caused a shift in the supplies, as well.

The first version of the website was in the late Fall of 2009, and I was fortunate enough to bargain with the boatyard. The boatyard's website was in dire need of some modernization, and since that is what I did as my regular day job, I approached the general manager to offer my services. In exchange for a website redesign and continued maintenance afterward, I asked if I could have a small presence on their new website—two pages with one for lessons and the other for charters. He agreed, and a contract was worked up and signed by both parties. I knew I would pro-vide sailing lessons and private charters, but they needed more detail. Under the category of lessons, I would have a twelve-hour beginner course, a sixteen-hour coastal cruising course, a five-hour adult refresher, and a private class by the hour—full price for the first and half price for a second person. Charters would consist of three-hour half-day, six-hour full-day, and three-hour evening events—fixed price for the group of up to five people. By the spring of 2010, I published their new website after they approved the design. Included in my pages were links to an availability calendar service I felt would suffice for the job of letting my customers know if and when I was available. I also had ties to the first version of a credit card service company, allowing me to start receiving online payments. Now that I had a web address that I can use on my marketing material, I could order rack cards and business cards to start the season. Initial fliers were designed and ready for emailing when necessary.

In April 2012, I changed cell phone vendors, and with that, I upgraded my phone to a smartphone. Apps for the smartphone will include three weather, two Doppler radar, tides, chart plotter, U.S. Coast Guard app, Google Sheets, Google Calendar, Google Analytics, and a credit card processing app. A single panel on my smartphone will contain all of these business-related apps, making it easy to find a specific app. Why three weather apps, you say? Not all weather predictions are the same, and if I see two that match for any given day, it will be my guide. I spent a good month evaluating weather apps to see which one was most accurate. I would note the forecast in each and then compare it with the historical weather data at the end of the day. The results led me to the three that I chose.

It's also good to have a weather app that shows hourly forecasts that include winds and gusts, temperature, and dew point. A note on the dew point, whenever the dew point gets within four degrees of the temperature, you get fog. With an hourly forecast, you can tell when fog arrives and when it will leave. Here in Maine, we deal with a lot of fog throughout the summer. Doppler radar is invaluable on the water as you would like to know what those dark clouds to the west are bringing. One does an excellent job showing very local radar, while the other showed a more expansive coverage area. Once I know where the scattered showers are going, I can generally sail around them. It's also good to see if you are in a quadrant of severe weather. There have been days when an approaching lighting storm cut the event short, so we returned early for pure safety.

One app that has become invaluable alerts me to fraud, scam, or spam; it immediately disconnects the call. This app has saved countless hours of unnecessary wasted time.

Part of the cellphone signup process was to define an email address, allowing me to have an email account dedicated to the business that would stand out, easy to say, and be understood when spoken and easy to remember. I wanted an email that was secure, free, synchronized with my email software, and available through my computer or smartphone. It did not take much thought on which service to go with and from which gosailing. cascobay@gmail.com was born. Going with a Google account for the business had so many more benefits. It gave me Google Drive for documents and spreadsheets, a YouTube channel for videos, and Google Analytics for my website. All devices reflect the same content through synchronization.

Unfortunately, the new email address caused the first change to the boatyard's website within my specific pages. The rack cards and business cards now needed to be tossed and reprinted with the new email address. I then needed to replace the rack cards in the two tourist visitor centers where they currently resided.

On the upside, the Gmail account allowed for yet another folder structure for the organization of emails. I created a customer folder for emails specific to customer correspondence and a follow-up folder for items needing further work. Tags allow me to refine the type of email further. I would generally keep just the latest email as long as the thread was present. The ability to search across emails was beneficial when I needed to locate a specific customer and their associated correspondence. I particularly appreciate the ability to add a customized signature in all replies. The signature is beneficial as another form of marketing, mostly when corresponding with noncustomers. The format for the signature includes my name, phone number, and website URL.

Since business emails will come through my Gmail account, I defined a unique notification sound on my smartphone, making it easier to differentiate the business emails from personal emails.

I also discovered that several hands-free smartphone apps would read your Google account emails and even allow you to send a reply verbally while driving.

May 2012 brought a significant life change as I fully retired from my day job as a web developer. It was an excellent career that served my family and me well for over 35 years. But now, I can devote all of my sailing season time to the business. I no longer needed to ask my manager for a day off when a customer signed up for a sail. Through 2010 and 2011, I used my six weeks of vacation time each summer for my customers.

In the winter of 2014, the management changed at the boatyard. They decided to change the website's focus solely on their business and not have a sailing business present, forcing me to create a new website dedicated to the sailing business that became version 2. It turned out to be a blessing, though, as I would have total control of the site and its ranking on the search engines and not share the internet space with a boatyard. The gosailing-cascobay.com URL was born during this period. The site took a few short months to design and publish, and once it was, I hid the two pages from the boatyard's website, leaving the underlying pages there. I coded an automatic jump to the new associated pages within the new site. The reason for this was to continue honoring the old reference that remained on the rack cards and other places that I still needed to locate and change. That took some time to find every internet site that referenced my original lesson and charter pages and get them to change it to the new address—another round of tossing the existing cards and have new ones updated and reprinted. It was amazing how far a web address will get in such a short time.

At the same time, I signed up with a new credit card processing service[27] dropping the original. The original vendor was too time-consuming to set up at the beginning of each season, which allowed me to rethink how I wanted to process online payments. Like before, the refund process had to be easy; internet and app available; quick links to my offerings; allowed customer lookup; modern card and chip reader with or without WiFi. The service that I found met all of my requirements; it was easy to set up and deposited directly into the business checking account. The card reader was ordered and arrived within a few days. To create my online marketplace, I needed to define my offerings and what I would charge for each. Making the online storefront was easy thanks to the service company's simple development tool, and it even offered links so I could add them to the website—another reason to go with this vendor. The new service served me well for the remainder of the business. Over the years of this service, I went through three versions of readers as the payment methods evolved from swipe followed by chip and, finally, contactless payments.

Having an entirely new website offered me the chance to check out the prices of my competition. I hadn't checked it since I opened the business. Given what I discovered, I made a few tweaks to my fees; the significant change was to have a fixed price for the first two people and fifty dollars for each additional person for my charters. The lessons increased slightly.

In the summer of 2015, I turned away many customers as my days filled up quickly. I felt terrible about this, and so I then started to consider taking on another captain. It did not take long to find one as I knew of just the right person who was also a member of the boatyard, Capt. Bill Babbitt, had his captain's license, and had a boat similar in size as mine. He was intrigued by my proposal when I asked, "Would you be interested in taking on my excess customers?" He was willing to do the charters but not the lessons as he didn't feel confident enough to teach sailing even though he helped many a crew when he raced. I was OK with that arrangement, and so our relationship began.

This change caused me to rethink the availability calendar. The current service[28] could not handle such a situation as it only offered available, reserved (which I changed to say closed), and booked. My thought was for any booked day where I am unavailable that I show a charter is still open but on Bill's boat, the Anie O'Dea, a thirty-one foot Catalina. Once he became unavailable, then the day is marked booked. The color scheme would change to introduce green on the charter calendar, which would indicate the customer would be sailing with Bill rather than me. In looking for a solution to this change, I could accomplish what I needed in a three-tab Google sheet. Using Google Sheets, I put together a three-tab sheet showing a simple calendar with color-coded dates. There is one tab for Lessons, one for Charters, and one for Evening Sails; I only needed to show the sailing months from May through October. I found a calendar template[29] that allowed me to show May through August in the first row, followed by September through December in the second row. I added a legend below the months, indicating that gray stands for closed, white (default) stands for available, green for the Anie O'Dea available, and red stands for "not available" (booked). The website will contain a link to a specific tab so a customer can quickly see what days I am available for the event they are inquiring about. Through Google Sheets on my smartphone or through the internet, I can update any day's status using the color scheme mentioned above. Keeping the calendar updated on a moment's notice is critical, as potential customers may simultaneously view my availability. In one instance, I had just changed the color of a given day, received a call moments later from a customer who was looking at the day I had just changed, and said, "The day I was viewing just changed? That was fast." As I am the only employee, I would then mark the Lesson tab for the same day as unavailable when a customer books a charter. The same is true for the opposite. Evening sails are standalone and do not affect the day events.

The beauty of this allowed me to control the day colors from my smartphone using the Google sheets app. There was an issue in the app version of sheets that forced me to select blue to fill a cell and have it appear red online. The problem did not happen if I made the change via a browser. It took a while to show Google tech support the issue and get them to agree that there was a problem. They fixed it after several days and a few emails.

July 2016 brought another significant change. As smartphones became more widely used, websites needed to respond to the smaller screen size. My current website did work on smaller screens, but I was not satisfied with the result, and I saw an increase in website visitors using smaller devices. I took this opportunity, which is how I see all changes, to redesign the entire website again. This version took less time than the last one, as I already had the text and images that I needed. All I had to do was transfer them to the new design. The new layout was much cleaner than the last one and easier to navigate. I was able to test the look and feel through all types of interfaces right on my local pc. I much prefer to view changes locally before I publish them to the web. I evaluated each page against the most common browsers, simulators for apple and android smartphones, and tablets. My goal here was to ensure the proper display of web pages—just a few necessary adjustments and ready to publish.

In January 2019, Google started pushing websites to have an SSL certificate and HTTPS designation. However, although not enforced, Google would mark your website as "Not Secure" and place your site lower in the search results. Obtaining the needed certificate was not difficult since the hosting company offered this at a small expense. Once they verified me as the domain owner, it took about four hours for the certificate installation on their end. Once I confirmed that the SSL was working, I resubmitted the website for reindexing by all search engines. One more modification was necessary on my website to force visitors using the HTTP to the HTTPS version, accomplished with a simple rule in the ".htaccess" file and republish to the hosting site.

Another internet search ensued to find all backlinks with the HTTP version of the web address and change them to the HTTPS version. A little tedious but necessary. The rack cards did not need to change as they didn't have either HTTP or HTTPS in the web address. If you ever put your web address on promotional material, you only need to show the domain name—no need to show "HTTPS://www." as modern browsers can handle the shorted URL just fine.

Also, in 2019 Maine legalized marijuana for recreational use; however, it was illegal on the waters patrolled by the U.S. Coast Guard. This development caused two changes, and one I needed from the Coast Guard. I asked them for the recommended wording of a drug-free vessel that I could post on my website, which they sent me. I also discovered a new warning placard in the marine store that I purchased and put on the Marisa III.

Marketing is another area where I have seen a lot of change throughout the business. These changes come from my own need to expand my reach, exploring unfamiliar options as I am new to the marketing world. I would have one core marketing company to promote me beyond the website and then add one experimental marketing campaign to see where it went. In the early years, I used the Maine Tourism Association. Still, I needed to change to another when they changed their technology, which resulted in the inability to find my business on their website. I asked them about this issue, and they could not resolve it. No problem, as the new core marketer[30] served me well for the remaining years.

For the experimental marking, I dedicated five hundred dollars a year. I placed an advertisement in one of the local weekly papers covering a sizable area that I served. I ran the ad during the peak months of July and August, which may have resulted in only a handful of customers. In the next year, I tried a radio ad with a local radio station writing a script based on a phrase my wife said once before we owned a boat, "Wouldn't it be nice to be out there sailing with the others on Casco Bay." The script was a thirty-second spot, and it took some adjustments to get it to fit in that time when spoken. The radio station liked the script without any changes and had two of their staff members say the parts since I wrote it as if a couple was looking out at the bay dreaming of sailing. The ad played twice each day for the entire season during the morning commute. Although I had several of my friends say they heard the ad, no one resulted in a customer, at least not that I knew. One year I signed up to be listed in the cruise line directory. Portland is a common stop for the various cruise lines throughout the Summer and Fall, some days having more than one in port at one time. From this experiment, I may have had two separate customers. The ships are just not in port long enough to result in passengers wanting to go out for a sail. They arrived mid to late morning and would leave early evening the same day.

Other experiments included sponsoring a play at a local community theater or donating two gift certificates per year to local auctions. I offered a discount to the Maine Island Trail Association members, which afforded me a link on their member benefits page. As a member myself, I placed a link to their website from mine. Whenever I found a link to my website from another website, I would reciprocate with a backlink to theirs. In doing that, both businesses benefit. Marketing companies, on occasion, would contact me offering to help promote my business. I had a standard phrase for these folks, "Thanks for the offer, but I can't handle any more customers." Available days diminished quickly as the years progressed, and I really could not take on any more customers. The days just kept filling up to the point where I would mark an occasional day as booked so that I could catch my breath. It's not easy to see the impact of a marketing campaign unless you ask, "How did you find me?"

As you can see, changes throughout the running of a business can be quite challenging and frequent. It is something that any business owner needs to keep on top of and not become complacent. Setting a fixed annual budget for marketing did help to keep me focused. It would have been too easy to go in too many directions at the same time. Just know that change happens, and if possible, don't let it stress you out.

9 LESSONS

From the moment I decided to start a sailing business, I knew it would include lessons. There have been several occasions in my life where I was a teacher, from ski instructor at a ski camp, conducting classes for adult education at a local high school, or substitute teaching at a public school, all gave me a thrill of teaching. I love seeing a student's excitement as an unfamiliar topic becomes familiar. The joy on their face is priceless when they feel accomplished.

With sailing, I wanted to combine a balance between instruction and hands-on experience. As long as a student is safe, I let them do something wrong, after which we would discuss what they just learned from the failed attempt. An example of doing something wrong is letting them get stuck in irons or having the wind backwind the headsail, blowing the bow to a new tack. Learning includes dealing with the many situations that they will experience, both good and bad, and getting themselves out of a problem benefits them in the long run. I am a firm believer that teaching should be low pressure. For any topic, the student should read it, hear it, see it and do it, and then as the teacher, you should observe, listen, and be patient. The students have enough to think about with the new sailing terms and sailing concepts in general. Indeed, they do not need someone pressuring them to learn. I have had students that have had to deal with these types of teachers; all gave them a bad experience. I can only hope that I helped relieve that painful memory and put the thrill of sailing back on their list of good memories.

Offering different sailing lessons seemed to meet the needs of students coming to me for various reasons. I designed the certificate courses as formal training while the private lessons, adult refresher, and standalone navigation course were more informal. Since all of my classes were private, I rarely had more than two students at any one time. Husbands have sent their wives to me for lessons, imagining this was easier on their marriage. Anyone under sixteen, I sent to the area sailing schools designed for kids on smaller boats. My granddaughter sailed the Marisa III at ten years old, but we needed to place cushions on the cockpit's sole so that she could see over the cabin top. A fond memory for my wife and me.

For the beginner course, I drew from my years of sailing and crafted the material for someone with no experience of sailing what so ever. Just enough to have them understand the concepts while sailing a thirty-foot sailboat. Starting slowly and building through the twelve hours while I had them aboard. I mailed the textbook early enough for them to have read the course material before they arrived for the first day of lessons. The day would begin in the cabin, they sitting on one side of the table and I on the other. I would ask them what their expectations were as they started their sailing adventure. Did they have any sailing experience? Some had ambitions of buying a sailboat for their family to enjoy, while others had loftier goals of sailing the world. Both had that same look of wistful anticipation. These initial conversations were all part of my getting to know them better and understanding how they handled learning; some more visual, while others are more verbal.

I started going over ten diagrams[31] laminated on 8.5x11 sheets of paper double-sided. I had pages one through five backed with pages six through ten in that order. Once I completed a diagram, I just slid it to the side, stacking them one through five with five on top. After the last diagram was complete, I turned the stack over, which now showed page six on top and ten on the bottom. The topics discussed included rules of the road, points of sail, the pecking order, sound signals, to name a few. With the sailing right of way topic, I used my homemade model sailboats and the wind direction arrow to make the lesson more visual. I positioned the boats in a converging situation and then placed the wind arrow pointing toward them. I then showed port and starboard tack, and given that, I then explained what should happen as they converged, applying the correct right of way rule. Over the two days, I reinforced the right of way rule whenever possible while underway, even when not close to another boat.

The final classroom-type topic was knot tying, and here I chose the most common knots to teach the students. Keeping one for myself, I gave each student a short line where they learned the stopper knot and square knot. Using my homemade knot tying board[32], a repurposed cutting board from home, they practiced the cleat hitch, clove hitch, and bowline knots. For the cleat and clove hitches, it was good to explain that these can be horizontal and vertical and why. I ended the classroom portion with an explanation of how the rest of the day would go.

Next, I took them on a boat tour, starting with the inside showing them the battery switch and electrical panel. I would turn on the day's necessary breakers. I showed them the VHF radio and demonstrated its operation using channel 27 for the automated radio check, life jackets, charts indicating where we were going to conduct the lessons, engine, and radar. Up on deck, I would discuss the winches and how the jib sheets were to be wrapped and locked as these winches were self-tailing. I continued with how the mainsheet worked, engine controls, outhaul, boom vang, and furler. While at the bow, I explained the mooring line and cast off procedures; here, I would ask for a volunteer to cast off. When there is only one student, that task was self-evident.

With the engine started and the volunteer at the bow, we cast off, and we are on our way motoring to the edge of the mooring field. Once we are clear of the twelve hundred boats bobbing on their moorings, I would ask, "Who wants to go first?" The first exercise was to get familiar with the tiller and boat's responsiveness. I have them motor a steady course using the bow against the shoreline in the distance as a guide, playing with the tiller, watching the bow react to the movement. I then would have them maneuver a sharp turn to port and again hold a straight course toward Clapboard Island. After a short distance, I issued a hard turn to starboard toward The Brothers, and after a while, perform a sharp 180-degree turn. They were always amazed at the boat's responsiveness as it could almost turn on itself, not the same as a powerboat.

The winds in Casco Bay over the summer months don't start to fill in until after eleven, which is why I start the course at ten. While the winds are still light, we raise the mainsail, and I take the helm showing them the boom's position using the main-sheet for each point of sail. I maneuver the boat through a tack and a jibe, and through the jibe, I have the student manage the mainsheet. We discuss the task beforehand, so they know what to expect and why. With two students, one will take the helm while the other handles the mainsheet, hard to center, then quick release. We go through each point of sail, focusing on the wind direction and location of the mainsail. I tell them that we want an even flow of air on both sides of the sail when upwind sailing, and to get that effect, we point the front of the sail into the wind. With downwind sailing, the concept changes. Here, we want the wind to hit the sail directly and boom perpendicular to the wind. I have them change roles and repeat the same points of sail. Once they get that concept, I pick a point of land that is upwind of us and have them sail to that reference, maximizing the close haul point of sail.

Completing this exercise, it is now close to lunch, so we take a break while I take the helm. We discuss what they have learned so far, and usually, they have lots of questions. It's an excellent time to get to know one another more since we still have a day and a half together. I tell them what the remainder of the day will consist of, and they relax to enjoy their lunch while I sail. There is a particular area of Casco Bay between Falmouth and Portland that is wonderful for teaching as this area has hardly any lobster buoys. Fewer obstacles to avoid, which will come later.

Now that lunch is over and the winds have settled in for the day, we open up the headsail to ninety percent. The reason for the shorted headsail is two-fold. First, it allows the student to see under the sail as the fully open genoa's foot scrapes the deck, resulting in no view on the bow's leeward side, and second, it's extended just enough for them to get the concept of changing tacks with both sails. Again, we go through each point of sail, along with tacking, jibing, and sailing to a reference point.

With any time remaining to the end of the day's lesson, I offer a period of free sailing. Here they can practice what they just learned or enjoy sailing around the small area of the bay. One tip I always share with new sailors is, "Never sail in winds stronger than the length of your boat and never go out in seas taller the one-quarter that its length."

The end of the day brings us back to the mooring, and my student volunteer is at the bow, ready to grab the stick as I approach the mooring. Together, we close up the boat for the day and discuss what tomorrow will bring. I call for our launch to get us back to the dock, and we call it a day. They covered quite a bit for a day, and I notice that their smile is a bit wider than when we started.

Day two starts with them readying the boat, covers removed and stowed below, seacocks opened, cushions brought up to the cockpit, electronics turned on, and the engine started. Before we cast off, I ask if they have any questions as they have had time to reflect on what they have experienced so far. With questions answered, they are excited to get going for their second day on the water. Like the day before, we start with some motoring drills. I begin by showing how far a boat will coast through the water at idle speed and neutral. I use two lobster buoys for this exercise; passing the first buoy, I idle back and shift to neutral and drift to the second buoy. The goal here is to see how far we drift from the first marker until the boat reaches one knot on the knot meter. I perform this task twice, once going upwind and once going downwind, and note the difference. This lesson leads us to an exercise in docking. I locate a mooring ball with a long pennant and a pickup stick, which becomes our simulated dock. Much better than practicing against something real and rigid. The concept is the same and much safer for the students and the boat. I show the students what I am looking for through a couple of passes, then turn the helm over to them, each taking several attempts. The drill works for docking as well as pulling up to a mooring.

Now the winds are filling in nicely; I have the student at the tiller head into the wind and raise the main. When I have two students, I will have one man the mainsheet while the other manages the steering. I will call out a point of sail and then have the student maneuver the boat to that reference while the other sets the main to the correct position. Each student runs the vessel through a few tacks and jibes. I am starting to see their confidence building. We add the headsail larger than the previous day but still not fully opened. After a few more tacks, we head for two more lobster buoys where the line between them is perpendicular to the wind, three boat lengths apart. I have them perform figure eights between them, going downwind of each, rounding up and tacking to the other. After I feel they get this concept, I explain the man overboard procedure. I explain that the buoy we just turned around is our victim, and we need to go to the second buoy, tack, and return downwind of our victim, round up to a close reach luffing the sails as we approach—one of the few good uses of a lobster buoy. There are not many. At this point, I take the helm and show them one more way to pick up a person who has fallen overboard. For this, I demonstrate heave to explaining that it only needs one person on board. I am always amazed at how many experienced sailors have not done this maneuver even though they have read about it—a great tool to add to your sailing resume.

It's now lunchtime and another opportunity to discuss what they have experienced so far. I tell them we need to be back at the mooring with enough time for them to take their test.

One topic I always impart to my students is how to balance the boat. What I mean by "balance" is with the right amount of sail exposed to the wind conditions, I should be able to let go of the tiller, and the boat will still hold its course. A sailboat will round up into the wind when there is too much sail area. She will turn away from the wind when there is not enough. Knowing this, you can then adjust the sail area and recheck the tiller by letting it go. Throughout the lesson, and anytime the winds change, while a student is at the helm, I will ask them, "Is the boat balanced?" The Marisa III would even balance on a close reach at twenty degrees of heel in a stiff breeze.

The remainder of the day is the free sailing time as they can take over the boat and go wherever they like within the bay's confines. I believe this is the student's most favorite time of the lesson since they have gained enough confidence with the boat to sail her as if it was just them, yet knowing I am there if they go astray.

Back at the mooring, I give them their test. The test consists of twenty-five appropriate multiple-choice questions[33] that I drew from the Coast Guard exam. The questions were either explained in their reading or through discussions over the two days on the water. For the first couple of years, I gave each student a test. I soon realized that I should offer one test for both to discuss and complete together. Since the two people, usually a married couple, will be more of a team, the change made sense and worked well for the remaining years. The answer sheet was a stock bubble answer sheet allowing fifty answers; bubbles marked A, B, C, D. To see how they did quickly, I took a sheet of mylar marking the place where the correct answers would appear when I overlayed the sheet with their marked answer sheet. Any incorrect answer became apparent, and I indicate on the bubble sheet where the answers were wrong. I would then go over the incorrect responses to see why the correct answer made more sense. Upon passing, I presented them with their printed certificates, prepared the night before.

The day ends with a feeling of accomplishment for them and me. They with visions of future sailing adventures, possibly taking the next lesson. Most schedule the next course right away, while some start looking for their first sailboat with hopes that I can offer more classes on their boat.

If it weren't for the islands in Casco Bay, I would not have crafted the Basic Coastal Cruising course the way I did. I wanted it focused on navigation as a follow-up class to the Beginner Sailing course. It starts with a three-hour study conducted in the boatyard's conference room; the first half is a PowerPoint presentation on navigation, twenty-eight pages in length, and the second half is hands-on problem-solving. I hook up my laptop to the large screen TV to make the presentation[34] more comfortable to see by the students at the table. Here they learn the tools used, chart symbols and scales, latitude and longitude, tides, currents, the compass rose, distance and bearing measurements, fixes, and solving for speed, time, and distance. As I speak to a topic in the presentation, I show live examples such as an actual full-size paper chart, a copy of a Booklet Chart for Casco Bay, the definitive book of chart symbols, dividers, and a parallel ruler, to name just a few.

In the second half of the class, the focus changes to the students. I hand out dividers, parallel rulers, soft erasers, pencils, a calculator, and a sample student work chart for solving the fifteen problems[35]. Bringing up the work chart on the TV, we review the parts it contains, such as the latitude and longitude scales, the buoys' location, lights, and the compass rose. I present the problems as a PowerPoint presentation in which we discuss what each is asking. Each shows four possible answers, which helps guide the student. Once they have the answer, one click of the mouse floats an arrow to the correct answer. I added a link labeled "Solution" that presents a PDF version of the work chart showing how to solve the specific problem when clicked. The solution becomes another point of discussion. We progress through the remaining exercises, which take a little more than an hour. The class's homework assignment is to plot a course from the mooring field around Long Island in Casco Bay and back. We will use their plot on the last day of the class. To help them with the assignment, I give them a divider, parallel ruler, and a printed copy of the chart showing the area they need to plot. I tell them that they should plot their course on the chart, but they should also list each leg in a table format to include the columns for name, bearing, distance, and a note.

The next day, the students meet me at the dock at ten to start their first on the water lesson. This day consists of running a course I plotted to sail from Falmouth South to Portland harbor, out Whitehead Passage around Peaks Island, and back through Hussey Sound and North of Cow Island.

When we get to the boat, we go below, review the plot, and work up a tide table for the time we will be sailing, recording high, low, and slack tides. Using the tide/current table for the day, we discuss the current speed and direction when sailing through Whitehead Passage and Hussey Sound. There have been times when we could only motorsail through as the winds were on the nose and we were fighting the current. We also check the hourly forecast to see which plot lines may need to be adjusted while underway. Whenever you plot a loop, indeed, one of the courses heads into the wind.

Once we get to the first mark on the plotted course, I take the helm with the sails up while the students tell me what bearing to steer as they also manage the sail trim. They use the chart as an overview guide but refer to the reference table of plot legs as they look for each mark on our journey. I have them calculate the time to the next spot now that we have an idea of our average speed via the knot meter. The table shows the distance. They make a note on the table, and we check the time when we reach the mark. We perform this same task on the first few legs.

When the next mark's bearing is impossible due to the wind direction, I have them plot a new course.

While underway, I take every opportunity to review the rights-of-way whenever another vessel is near enough to cause concern. I will ask, pointing to the other boat, "Who has the right-of-way and why?" With the answer complete, we take the appropriate course of action. Sailing through Portland harbor is always a challenge, given the activity that is common there.

Over the years of sailing Casco Bay, I have learned how to determine the wind speed by looking at the water surface. When I first see the occasional whitecaps, I know the wind around ten miles per hour (mph). Fifteen mph is when I see ribbons of white bubbles streaming into the wind. When the whitecaps are more numerous and breaking, we are looking at twenty. It just gets worse after that.

As we continue through our loop, I will point out some of the many hazards lying below the surface and show how they appear on the chart. I show them how the current reveals itself by observing a nearby lobster buoy—the second use of these sea obstacles. Looking at the wake made by the current, you will see the direction and get an idea of the strength, leading to a discussion of set and drift. To see if the current impacts my course, I line up two lobster buoys and watch the result. If the near buoy moves left of the far one, I am drifting to starboard. If the near one moves right, I am sliding to port. From this, I adjust my bearing until another pair of buoys stay in line, the boat diagonal to the course line.

With loop completed, if there is any time remaining at the end of the day, I let the students take over the helm and sail as they wish until our time is up.

Back at the mooring, we discuss the day and what tomorrow will entail. They will need to bring their plotted course, two hourly forecasts from separate sources, and the navigation tools they borrowed—another accomplished day.

On day two, we gather in the boat's cabin and review the plot by the students. I check their bearings and distances for any errors and look for any tracks that cross hazards. In going over the weather reports, we get a sense of what we will be dealing with and discuss sail plans. The students have the choice to go around Long Island clockwise or counterclockwise. The day's wind direction helps them decide. When the winds are out of the East, it isn't easy to get out of Chandler's Cove.

With everyone in agreement, we cast off, and our day commences. The students take over the running of the boat for the day while I watch. For the times when I have only one student, we will alternate taking the helm and trimming. Since releasing the jib sheet from the winch can be accomplished with one hand, the person who will do the releasing takes the tiller, tacking the boat.

The other person needs both hands to trim the jib to the other side.

An advantage of having a tiller is I can tack and trim the jib single-handed. I straddle the tiller leaving both hands free to handle the sheets. A few turns around the windward winch taking out any slack. A shift of my body to leeward starts the turn. The leeward sheet is unwrapped from the winch but held until I see a backwinded jib. Sheet released, sail starts its shift to the other side, now both hands are free and used to trim the jib, shift my body to center heading for the new course.

On one occasion, the fog rolled in the night before and expected to stay the entire day, visibility well under a quarter-mile and no wind. As this was the second day, and we were going to run his course, I gave him the option to motor the whole route or reschedule the lesson. His decision to run it in the fog started a new discussion on dealing with foggy days. We reviewed the sound signals we will need to listen for and broadcast. I started up the radar, and we went over its functionality, raised the radar reflector to the starboard spreader, fired up the handheld GPS. We cast off and motored at three knots going from point to point, buoy to buoy through the entire loop. We calculated each leg's time, so when we got close to our mark, we each would attempt to spot it in the fog. We felt accomplished each time we did, high five, and it was off to the next point. Eleven miles and three hours later, we completed the loop.

The day ends back at the mooring as I pass out the thirty-two multiple-choice test[36], a set of dividers, parallel ruler, calculator, a sample chart, and leave the students on their own while I closed up the boat. Test complete, checked, and reviewed, handed out the certificates, and the launch takes us back to the dock.

At this point in their training, they have the option of private lessons or a five-hour adult refresher course. These help to focus on and improve skills. A typical scenario is that the students will buy a boat and hire me for the refresher course, which allows them to gain confidence in their vessel. We spend the initial time going over what their boat has for equipment and the rigging, noting each line's purpose. On the water, we run through all the maneuvers that they had experienced during the beginner course seeing how their boat handles. I leave them feeling that their investment will give them years of memories. It is now up to them to expose themselves to various weather conditions and to explore Casco Bay to its fullest.

Teaching sailing on another person's boat is a treat for me. Not only do I get to help someone else with their skills, but I also get to sail on a vessel that I would typically never get to do. Over the past ten years, I have taught a couple with no sailing experience on their forty-foot Island Packet. They now are sailing the world, and the last time I checked their blog, they were in South America. I helped another experienced sailor on his fifty-footer to become familiar with Quahog Bay and the area islands as he and his wife recently moved to the area from Florida. I crewed with a father and son as they delivered their sailboat from Wells to Portland; in pea soup fog no less. Fortunately, I had plotted a course the night before, just in case. It was clear skies when we left, and the fog rolled in with a vengeance early in the day. The remainder of the day was motoring from one buoy to the next along the coast. Once we reached Portland harbor, the fog disappeared. That's Maine for you.

Generally, lessons amounted to forty percent of my business each summer, yet it gave me at least sixty percent satisfaction as compared to charters. There is so much pleasure in teaching sailing. To have the student take those lessons to heart in such a way as to become their new passion. A passion that I have carried throughout my entire life.

Many a day ended with a one hour break before meeting my next customers arriving for an evening sail.

10 CHARTERS

The majority of my business consisted of taking folks out for a sail without a lesson's formality. The people came from all over the country, from families vacationing in Maine, locals seeking a thrill of sailing, couples wishing to share a memory or special occasion. Each had the same look when they arrived at the dock. Some had sailed before; most had not. To the ones that were new to sailing, their excitement was infectious; they could not get enough of the adventure, eyes wide with anticipation.

Again, I got pretty good at knowing who my customers were as they walked down to the dock. They had that quizzical expression when you are trying to find someone. I would approach them as they neared and ask if they were the Allens, Martins, Jennifer, or Mark as an example of our initial greeting. Rarely would I get a response of, "No, sorry." If they had not paid for the event beforehand, they would usually ask if they should pay now. I would say, "Let's settle up at the end." I wanted them to experience the time on the water before I asked for payment. It was always better that way, and their thank you came in smiles and the occasional tip.

"Ready to go?" I would ask, and it was off to the launch, which delivered us to the Marisa III and their adventure.

It's a short ride from the dock, and once we are all on board, I started to ready the boat. I open the lock, slide the hatch, remove the two chestnut-colored panels to the companionway, placing them below, after which I would begin to pass the three cushions for the cockpit to the passengers, which were like puzzle pieces as they put them in their proper location. I returned to the cockpit to remove the covers from the tiller, winches, knot meter, and compass putting them down in the cabin space. While below, I would turn on the electronics, open seacocks, and ask if my passengers wanted any of their gear placed in the cabin. As they passed me their bags and coolers, I put the heavy items on the cabin sole, lighter items on the settee. By this time, the people have found their spot to sit, and conversations began to escalate. Back in the cockpit, I pass the flag to someone to place on the stern. When the winds are agreeable for full sails, I ready the main by taking the sail cover off and asking someone to stow it in the cabin while I attach the halyard to the headboard. On the bow, I prepare the mooring line for a quick cast off. I start the engine and mention where I like to sit; on the starboard cowl near the winch, giving me the best vantage as I can see alongside the boat and be near the furling line and sheets. I am right-handed; however, I seem to like handling the tiller with my left. Come to think of it, I play pool left-handed. Weird. Casting off complete, we motor out of the mooring field for our day together on Casco Bay.

For the first couple of years in business, I would take up to six passengers, the maximum allowed for my license. It didn't take long to realize that six was too much for the boat, causing me to stand the entire time, so I changed it down to five. Much more comfortable and manageable. Invariably, I would get calls from folks asking me if I could take out more than five, some as large as twelve. I would have to say no and then direct them to my web site's FAQ page, where I offer alternatives for large groups with links.

Once away from the crowded anchorage, I ready the sails from the cockpit. When I have the mainsail in the day's sail plan, I idle the engine and head the boat into the wind. I can raise the sail from the cockpit while keeping the tiller snug to my leg. The customers' look is priceless, with their eyes widening on each pull on the main halyard watching the sail rise to the top of the mast. I bear away and cut the engine. A hush engulfs the Marisa III as I allow the wind to fill the sail. "Best sound in the world," I say as I look at my passengers beaming. Sailing close haul, I put a few turns of the jib sheet around the winch with my left hand and start to open the headsail using the furling line with my right. Once fully open, I take in the slack on the sheet, lock it in place in the self tailer, and trim with the winch handle. The Marisa III kicks into high gear as the wind hits the headsail. The boat starts to heel to leeward; passengers not sure what to expect, and I am sure they think we will tip over. I point out the clinometer at the base of the companionway, explaining its purpose. As the passengers look at the gauge, I will invariably get the question, "How much is too much?" I reply with, "I always measure too much by the whites of the eyes. People panic well before the boat does." The reply will cause a laugh, and they relax a bit. My wife's favorite is five knots, ten degrees. To the most nervous person aboard, I show them the mainsheet and teach them how releasing it will level the boat, usually taking five degrees off the heel. They gain some confidence knowing they can control the heel, and I acquire a crew member.

On breezy days, I will unfurl just the one-thirty genoa. She has a good shape, fully opened or furled to eighty percent depending on the wind speed. The boat does well with this sail plan to the amazement of some experienced passengers. It does not take much sail, or wind, to move a Pearson 30. Just because you have the sails doesn't mean you have to use them or to their fullest. It is a matter of balancing the boat.

At this point, I will ask if anyone aboard would like to help. Not required, but I feel everyone should at least have the opportunity. For those who say yes, I give them a crash course on handling the jib sheet and winch handle on the winch. The winches are two-speed self-tailing types; hard and fast in one direction, easy and slow in the other. Some will ask if they can steer. Of course, I say yes. So lovely to have a new crew for the day. It wouldn't be the first time where new to sailing folks want to continue the experience.

Route options are plenty, and while preparing the boat for the day, I watch the wind speed and direction. These two indicators will help me to decide what the route will be for the day. The route choice is also dependent on whether the event is a half-day, full-day, or evening sail, time being the central concern, three hours, six hours, three hours, respectively.

The most common route is to sail directly from Falmouth deep into Portland harbor and back. With favorable winds, I will return by sailing through Diamond Pass between the islands of Great Diamond and Peaks. This area offers beautiful shorelines that are typical in Maine. Great photo opportunities for the passengers. The Casco Bay ferry will often pass nearby, and I'll have my passengers get the tourists' attention on the ferry and get them to wave, just checking to see if they are paying attention to us. "Oh, look. Someone is taking your picture," to which my passengers wave even more vigorously.

On the northern end of Diamond Pass, I can take a shortcut further into the bay, but the winds must be right to do this route, forming the letter "Z ." If the winds are out of the South, I will turn the boat toward the green can number one between Crow and Great Diamond. When I get close to the right spot, I turn to starboard for a short distance and then port and head for the number two nun between Cow and Great Diamond, completing the zigzag. The depth at low tide is twelve feet as long as I stay mid-channel between Cow and Great Diamond. Three legs, two jibes, and we are through. What's pleasant for the passengers is how close we come to the shoreline—a short but fun adventure.

It's a treat when the winds are out of the West, allowing for a straight run out to the Portland Headlight. This historic landmark is one of the most photographed lighthouses in the country and to see it from the water is a must.

There is a lot of history between Falmouth and Portland, so much so that I printed and laminated a few history cards, keeping them at an easy reach while aboard. I'll pass the set to one of the passengers to read to the group while I point to each historical reference. The cards include Fort Gorges, Mackworth Island, Spring Point Light, Eastern Promanade, to name a few.

Another route will take me East to Cousins Island, passing West of Basket Island, then across the bay to Great Chebeague. From there, with a favorable wind direction, it's five miles to

Mackworth Island.

People will ask the names of the islands that we see, of which I will name the ten or so that are visible in our periphery. With over two hundred twenty islands in Casco Bay, one can be overwhelmed. At that point, I'll duck down below and grab the chart and then pass it to someone, pointing to where we are, and show them some of the islands they are seeing. "This one is that, and this one is over there." The islands tend to blur together in the distance. Now they can follow along as we sail around the bay. Sometimes they will ask what the symbols mean, which leads to a discussion of how to read a chart.

When someone asks about the sea life they might see during their time aboard, I explain a game that I created to amuse the kids. For every seal that they spy, they get one point; a porpoise is worth five. For every seal they see that turns out to be a lobster buoy, they lose a point, and yes, I have had people go negative. The most seals seen in one day was twenty-three. No shark sightings, thank goodness. As in the movie Jaws, I hope I never have to say, "I think we need a bigger boat." One day on the oceanside of Peaks, we saw a large fin lazily moving through the water with a slight floppy motion. Curious, we sailed over to see what it might be, and to our surprise, it was a gigantic ocean sunfish swimming sideways as they do, without a care in the world.

With a full day sail and six hours to play with, my routes become larger encompassing more islands to navigate. Since I ask that the passengers pack a lunch, I select a destination for our break sometime around one o'clock. My favorite is to sail East ten miles to a group of islands called the Goslings. I navigate to the East of Irony Island, drop the sails, turn on the engine, and motor to a place between West and East Gosling Islands. There I pick up one of the public moorings for our short stay. Here the passengers can relax while they enjoy their lunch. Some will ask if they can swim off the boat. To accommodate their wish, I put the swim ladder off the stern and say, "The pool is now open." They may swim just around the boat or venture to the nearby island to explore the sandy beach. After lunch, I choose which way I want to travel while we head home. Sailing back the way we came is frequent due to the wind direction, but there are times when I can cruise along the South-East shore of Great Chebeague, passing through Chandlers Cove and back to Falmouth.

For the full-day passengers who wish to see lighthouses, my route takes me out to the ocean through Hussey Sound, sail to Two Lights in Scarborough, then back into Portland Harbor, passing Ram Island light, Portland Headlight, Spring Point, and Bug Light. Passing the schooners that frequent the harbor is an added treat for the passengers and a chance for some great photos. Before heading back to Falmouth, I take them deep into Portland Harbor to view the working waterfront, passing lobster pounds, Portland's fishing fleet, chandleries, and some of the city's most valuable real estate.

Whenever I am sailing about two miles offshore and crossing the Portland Headlight navigation sector lights, I will say to the passengers to keep an eye on the lighthouse's base. With the shore to our starboard, I say, "Let me know when you see a red light." Once they see it, I'll say, "Let me know when it turns white." Then we look for the white to turn green. We then discuss what they just saw, explaining that ships coming into Portland Harbor look for the white light. When they do, they know they are on safe passage to the lighthouse. When they see red, they need to steer to port; green means turn to starboard. My passengers are always impressed with this little bit of navigation knowledge. The kids treat this as a game and compete to see who can see the lights first.

Whenever I can, I enjoy going out to Eagle Island, the home of Admiral Peary, now a state park. This island is on the outer edge of Casco Bay at the entrance to Broad Sound, about ten miles from the mooring. I will pull up to the dock, leaving them to explore the Peary house and surrounding island for up to two hours, the state park's maximum allowed. I tell them as they disembark to have the dock attendant shuttle them back to my boat when they finish their tour. While my passengers explore the island, I motor out to one of the available mooring balls available to the island's visitors, giving me the chance to enjoy a peaceful lunch while my passengers make some memories. My passengers return full of stories and excited to view a piece of American history. We plan our return route, of which we have a few choices.

Through the years, I have had charters get scheduled with the intent of a lesson. Some folks wish to explore what sailing is all about, a precursor to future, more formal training, while others use the charter to enhance what they already know. A boyfriend/girlfriend will do a lesson to share an experience in learning together. Parents will bring their children, asking me to give them a taste of sailing while they watch in amazement as their kids take to sailing right away. They may have a sailboat of their own or maybe planning on buying one soon. I will usually get the parents involved in the lesson to see how they work together as a team and offering them a chance to bond with their child. I had a couple bring their two teenage grandkids, Megan sixteen, Mathew fourteen, asking me to teach the kids the fundamentals of sailing while they beamed. Other times it is a family who will say they have never been on a sailboat before but would like to help crew the boat, resulting in wide eyes and enormous smiles ending with, "We had no idea it would be this much fun."

Some of my customers return each year, allowing us to reconnect and catch up with their lives over the prior year. Their reasons vary. They may be doing the annual sailing tradition while on vacation, or if local, a way to get out on the bay. I will note routes taken so if they return, I can take them to a new area they have yet to see. Others see it as an alternative to owning a boat of their own, and they budget accordingly. One customer has come out fifty-six times over seven years, and we are now close friends.

I am always amazed at the variety of food that people will bring aboard for their day's snack, lunch, or dinner. I have seen french picnics with exotic wines and cheeses, homemade sandwiches from the local sandwich shop, all kinds of fruit and nuts, juices, sodas, chips, to list just a few. I have had passengers ask me what I would like for lunch when they book, which is a nice treat. I keep ginger ale and bottled water aboard along with trail mix for anyone who gets hungry or thirsty. Dehydration is something I always watch for in my passengers. For those chilly days on the water, I have packets of hot chocolate and individual coffees to help warm the body. I also keep two blankets in the cabin and offer them to my passengers when I see them starting to show signs of being chilled.

Besides the personal questions that I get from my passengers, I will get a memorable one once in a while. One passenger a while back who asked with a straight face, "Those houses there along the shore, do they lose their view in the winter?" Not sure if she was joking, I paused a while before I responded with, "No. Why do you ask?" Her answer: "Aren't they all coated in snow?" I am not sure what National Geographic special she watched, but I had to say no, they do not lose their view. On a bright summer day, I had a North Carolina passenger ask, "How do you get your skies so blue?" You gotta love people *"from away."*

I have read that ocean air is good for your health, and I had one charter that was a testament to this theory. A couple booked a half-day sail with their twenty-six-year-old daughter, who has a lung condition. A Boston doctor had recently recommended ocean air therapy, so the parents would take their daughter to several East Coast locations for short vacations even though they lived in Ohio. When they arrived at the dock on a warm summer day, Heather was pale, but I could see that she was already taking in the salt air. The day included a gentle breeze, and we sailed all over Casco Bay while Heather sat on the bow. Her parents explained her condition and were hopeful that the three hours on the water would help their daughter. Indeed it did. By the end of the sail, Heather had much of her color back, and she was beaming with joy. She even said, "Casco Bay has the best air on the East Coast." I must admit that whenever I am on the water, I feel less stressed and relaxed.

Charters have been part of several celebrations such as birthdays, anniversaries, wedding parties, bridesmaid outings, and on one occasion, a wedding proposal. The wedding proposal is a great memory for me years later. I got a call from the bride-to-be's sister saying what she and her sister's boyfriend were planning. It was an elaborate plan culminating on a sunset sail including champagne. Everything fell into place quickly, and when the day arrived along with the young couple meeting me at the dock, I could see he was quite nervous; she did not have a clue. Her entire family and his all knew what was going to happen. Everyone at the boatyard knew as well and kept their poker faces on. I can not imagine what was happening at home while they waited patiently for word that this young couple from Boston were engaged. The sun on its descent was causing the clouds to turn pink and orange; she asked if she could sit upon the bow, to which I said, "Absolutely." She slowly went to the front of the boat and seated herself with her back against the cabin top, taking in the soft sounds and the setting sun. The young man, now a nervous wreck back with me in the cockpit, says, "Should I do it now?" "Good a time as any, I guess," I replied, knowing what was coming next. As he slowly moved forward to be with his future bride, I turned the boat into the setting sun, reflecting its glow on the water. He sat down next to her, took her hand, and with his other showed her the ring saying the words we have heard so many times before. I did not hear her reply, but I am sure of what it was when she wrapped her arms around her now fiance and gave him a huge kiss. He then got out his phone to call everyone waiting at home, and I did hear the cheers coming out of the phone. Returning to the cockpit, he surprised her further with the champagne chilling on ice in the cabin hidden in the ice chest. When we returned to the dock, the dock staff gave them a round of applause and congratulations. The couple returned the following year to celebrate their first anniversary, still as happy as the day I met them. So happy for them both.

When I started the business, I advertised "sunset sail" but soon changed it to evening sail when someone complained that they did not get to see the sunset. The "evening sail" was five to eight, yet depending on the time of year, the sun did not set until much later. Changing the wording seemed to alleviate that issue. By mid-August, the sun is starting to set around seven-thirty, so I mark the calendar as closed from that date forward. In the web site's Evening Sail section, I show the sunset time for the current date. I offer a link to a sunset table for the Portland area, telling them that if they want an evening sail, find the time of sunset for the day they want, and the start time will be three and one-half hours before that time. They can then request a half-day sail ending just before sunset. That has worked out well over the years.

An evening sail is very different than a day sail. The winds are lighter, and the air is cooler. The best time is when I have cloudless skies, and the full moon is just above the horizon while the sun sets in the West. Nothing beats dinner while sailing on a gentle breeze as the sky turns into its evening colors. For this, I will heave to the boat so they can enjoy their meal in peace. At least twice a week, we have to navigate around the area yacht races, but it's nice to see their spinnakers flying, so majestic. It's best when we return before the end of the race or well after. If we arrive at the mooring simultaneously, we may be waiting while the launch service brings the racers from their boats to the dock. I make the call on the radio for a pickup and have them say they will get us on the return trip, only to have them pass us with a full boat. "Get you on the next run." they'll say as they motor by. I have waited up to forty-five minutes for a pickup, but the customers don't seem to mind as they enjoy sitting and chatting in the cockpit listening to the windchime like sounds of the various halyards slapping against their masts.

Coming back once in the dark, past the time when the launch service ended for the night, I dropped my passengers off at the dock. I then asked them to hand me the painter for the boatyard's spare dinghy, thanked them, and said our goodbyes, motored out to my mooring—a good challenge in the dark but doable using my handheld spotlight. Once the boat was closed up for the night, I got myself into the dinghy and rowed back to the dock. Each pull on the oars activated the water's phosphorescence, resembling a sea of stars making everything glow nearby—such a sight to behold. Mesmerizing.

You can imagine that weather plays a significant portion in

sailing, and the wind is by far the most pronounced. However, there are days when the wind dies. While we drift for a while, waiting for the wind to decide what it wants to do, I will share my belief that there are gremlins who turn off the wind machines for no apparent reason, move them to a new location, then turn them back on. True enough, after twenty or so minutes of sitting with the tiller hard to one side of the boat, the wind returns, and we trim the sails and continue on our journey.

Pocket sailing is the term I give when the wind appears in small areas of the bay. Between these patches of air, the water is like glass and windless. Sails up, I will motor into a large pocket of wind, kill the engine and sail within the edges of wind, tacking when we get close to the edge. My customers are surprised by this phenomenon, thinking wind blows across the entire area, not in small patches.

One of the bay's benefits is its protection from the ocean swells, although I had one couple who were experienced lake sailors wanting to see what ocean sailing was all about. I am not sure if they picked the day they did on purpose or by chance. That day, there was a storm well out in the Atlantic, but the weather was pleasant in Falmouth. The plan was to take them out to the ocean through Hussey Sound as the winds were out of the East at fifteen. The first part of the trip was with no problems, the customers enjoyed the boat's motion, and we entered the Hussey, port tack, close reach. At that point, the Marisa III started to rise and fall, with the incoming swells gaining height the further we went. By the time we reached the Southside of the sound, the waves were between five and ten feet. In the troughs, the shoreline and horizon utterly disappeared. The eyes of my customers were as big as they could be, and they said, "That's enough ocean sailing. We want to go back to the lake." With the winds now more robust in the open, I had a tough time tacking the boat and navigating the swells, not enough momentum. I turned the engine on, waited for the vessel to reach the top of the wave, push the throttle, and quickly turned to port then down the backside —starboard tack, broad reach back into the bay. The customers relaxed a bit, happy to be back into calmer waters; I have not seen them since.

The fog has unique qualities for those who enjoy the intrigue of not knowing by sight where you are while you sail along. When temperature gets too close to dew point, they hide their relationship in fog only to clear when they go separate ways. I had four women from New Mexico arrive on one of the foggiest days in August. As we looked out at the thick cloud of white, barely seeing only a few near boats in the mooring field, I gave them the option to cancel or reschedule. As they had never seen fog before, they opted for going out for the sail. So off we went into the pea-soup fog, they on the bow, me in the cockpit with my GPS, radar, and compass. I would sail near the shore when I could and say, "Over here, you would see..." At one point, I could just make out one of the schooners from Portland, so I sailed over to her for a better look. As we got closer, she looked like a pirate ship coming through the fog to the glee of my passengers. Every once in a while, they would lean back and ask, "You sure you know where are going?" To which I would reply, "Sure. No problem." I would head over to any of the navigational buoys asking them to keep a lookout for the specific one I would describe. There would be one who spots it first, yell out and point, "Over there!" Upon returning to the dock, they could not say enough how much fun they had, sailing in the fog. A story I am sure they have shared many times.

One strange day, a fog bank rolled in from the ocean but not in the usual way. It was a bright sunny day when a fog line formed from Long Island to Clapboard, one-hundred feet tall, creating a distinct wall. North of this line was the densest fog as I have ever seen, yet South of this fog bank was bright full sun. I could sail right up to the wall, travel along its edge. Another sailboat came up alongside me, asking, "What is that doing?" After I said, "Nothing." they turned around and headed back to Portland. This wall stayed there for the entire day, not moving at all. Imagine the surprise when boats in the fog came out through the wall to such a dramatic change. To that, I still sounded my fog horn when we were close to the edge, not knowing what was on the other side, for they could not see us on the outside.

Over the years, I will say that I have not had to deal with rain too often as most people rescheduled or just canceled due to the weather. One family of four showed up to the dock for their half-day sail while the skies were getting dark to the West. Pointing to the skies, I asked them what they wanted to do. They looked at each other briefly, and then the father said, "We won't melt." OK then, off we go. At the point of motoring to the edge of the mooring field, the sky opened up, dropping hailstones the size of M&Ms. The splash they made in the water rose a foot or more. The family quickly ducked down into the cabin, looking out the cabin windows, the sound deafening as the hail pelted the deck; I ducked under the dodger because they hurt. The father soon then asked if they could reschedule. With luck, the next day was still available, which turned out to be a great day for everyone. I can only remember one other time when a storm came through mid-day, lightning included. Fortunately, we were not too far from the mooring field, dropped sails, and motored home. The first clap of thunder was our alert, and the doppler radar was the confirmation. I'd rather not sail with customers in my boat having a forty-five-foot lightning rod.

Even hot summer days can be a challenge, especially with young children. I remember one such day when a young couple brought their two-year-old with them. He looked so cute with his life jacket; however, the same item made him quite fussy. The heat and humidity were oppressive, as I recall. The parents were trying their best to calm the little one with no success. I asked the father to take the tiller while I went below to get the plastic pail from the V-birth. Bringing it back to the cockpit, I threw the bucket overboard, still holding on to the attached line. I placed the pail on the cockpit floor and suggested that their son could now play in the cool ocean water. Sitting next to the bucket, playing with the water, his squeals of delight put smiles on his parent's faces, and they even took the opportunity to put their hands into the bucket as well. They relaxed and enjoyed the sweltering and sticky day on the waters of Casco Bay.

A note about having young children aboard: I realize that kids can have short attention spans and little interest in the sailing experience. To that end, I always had activity books, crayons, the card game Fish, and a small whiteboard with dry-erase markers available for them to use to their heart's content. It truly helped on many a day for the kids and the adults.

Cancelations are something every business needs to deal with, and I am probably more forgiving than most. I know that life happens, and things change, so I don't hold it against customers who need to cancel. One couple had to cancel because they had nowhere to put their dog. Another couple from Kentucky had me waiting at the dock for about thirty minutes past their start time. At that point, I thought I would give them a call to see what was up. Maybe they forgot or were delayed in getting to me. Nope, they answered the phone after a few short rings and said they had decided not to go on vacation and stayed home. Some people will amaze you in unexpected ways. The day was beautiful, and the winds were calling me to play. I could not refuse.

Charters were a fantastic way to meet so many new people, each sharing the stories of their lives, and in return, I hope I gave them memories to share with their family and friends for years to come. Even though we meet as strangers, we leave as friends.

11 FINAL YEAR

Little did I know what 2020 would bring. It started as any typical year with a few early bookings from the holiday season. The news contained something about a virus spreading in China similar to the SARS virus from 2004, nothing to fret over.

I updated the website, offering my annual preseason discount during February. From this, I acquired a handful of initial bookings, some for May, June, and August. My repeat customers know to wait for this seasonal discount and take advantage when it appears. In February, the news was starting to show the virus, now called coronavirus, was beginning to occur outside of China, mostly still in the Asian countries. However, there were fourteen cases in the United States.

This year, my wife and I stayed in Tennessee as part of our annual winter getaway, expecting to return to Maine on March 16. By the beginning of March, the news was consuming more airtime with the coronavirus's progression worldwide. On March 11, the World Health Organization (WHO) declared that COVID-19, the coronavirus's latest name, as a pandemic. At this point, we started to wonder what our options were and whether we should go back sooner. Our choice became clearer when on March 12, our Governor in Maine confirmed its first case and began to apply restrictions within the state. We needed to get home before being trapped in Tennessee. If we were to get sick, we would rather be at home. Planning our return route, we noticed that the only state without any confirmed cases was West Virginia, so that was to be our first overnight. The next morning we packed up the car, notified the chalet owner, and headed for our first destination. It was sad to leave our home away from home that gave us so many restful weeks away.

The next morning we had planned to drive six hours, which would put us somewhere in Connecticut. As we traveled around New York City's outskirts, we heard of an outbreak in New Rochelle, a borough on our route. More states were reporting active cases. We reached Connecticut in the early evening, made a stop for a bite after a daylong drive. Sitting there, we decided to drive straight through to Maine, not wanting to stay another night in a hotel, just three more hours. Finally home and exhausted, we dropped our luggage and called it a night, not even bothering to unpack.

Two days later, Governor Janet Mills declared a civil state of emergency and started to implement lockdown measures to slow the spread of COVID-19 in Maine. All non-essential businesses and public-facing operations were to close their physical locations. Quite a blow to the companies in Maine, not knowing where this was going. The boatyard had to close its facility to the public, so they put up a sign at the entrance stating "Closed to the Public." Everything came to a screeching halt, and uncertainty was the feeling facing small business owners like myself.

By the end of March, the Governor issued a stay-at-home order for Maine residents, unless to leave for an essential job or a necessary activity such a groceries. Hiking trails remained opened so people could get outdoors for some fresh air and improve their well-being.

April brought several changes to our situation, including allowing out of state visitors from specific states as long as they self quarantined for fourteen days. A sign that Maine may be able to open up to our much-needed tourists. A promising sign for any sailing business. The federal CARES Act passed, allowing for an additional six hundred dollars for unemployment claims. It wasn't until the end of April that the self-employed could file for unemployment through the Pandemic Unemployment Assistance (PUA) program. As I was not sure when, or if, my business would be able to open, I filed for unemployment for the first time in my life, with hopes of recouping some of the expenses that I already had in preparing for the season. My application got approved for the minimum allowed plus the additional six hundred dollars from the federal government beginning May 1. I opted for the maximum state and federal taxes from my benefit to improve my tax filing next Spring. As long as I filed my weekly certification, I would continue to receive my weekly payment.

Governor Mills extended the state of civil emergency to May 15 and announced plans for the gradual reopening of Maine's economy. There were four stages defined with outdoor recreation, such a charter boats and boat excursions in phase three scheduled for July 1, although there was no date when the guidelines for them would be available. My first sign of hope.

In late April, I started to ready the Marisa III for the season and scheduled her launch date for May 15. The website needed a change to alert visitors that I had a tentative opening date of July 1 due to COVID-19 and that I would not offer lessons on another person's vessel. I put the words "ON HOLD" across each availability calendar and reduced my capacity to two people even though the guidelines said I could take up to six. For social distancing, I chose two. To the customers already booked in May and June, I sent them an email telling them of my plans, offering them rescheduling options when I did open or request a refund. All but one opted for rescheduling. A feeling of discomfort stayed with me each day as I wondered if I would be able to open the business at all. So much was changing as the virus spread across the country.

In early May, the Economic Recovery Committee was created with weekly public Zoom meetings frequently attended by our Governor. The committee was under the Maine Department of Economic and Community Development (DECD), with Heather Johnson as its commissioner. At times, the Zoom meetings had over five hundred businesses seeking answers to the many questions we had regarding the various company openings. We were glued to the hour-plus gathering, soaking in all the information we could deduce from the experts who were in control of our livelihood. Within this, we heard which businesses were to be in each stage of reopening, and each's guidelines. At times, it felt like a moving target, and for me, hoping to hear anything relating to the marine industries and outdoor recreation.

The Department of Maine Tourism began their own set of public Zoom sessions every week, letting us know how our state restrictions affected our tourists. It was hard to listen to the various businesses' questions, so dependent on the tourists and getting more desperate as time went on. The Canadian border closed, so there would be no tourists from our northern neighbor. The number of states allowed into Maine was changing as those states battled their infection rates. Maine lodging providers could begin accepting future reservations for stays with an arrival date of June 1 and beyond for Maine residents and non-residents who comply with the 14-day quarantine requirement. So much of my business depended on these tourists who come to vacation in our beautiful state. Some of our counties could reopen sooner than others; Cumberland, the location of my business, was in the latter category as the infection rate was still too high.

Near the end of May, state and federal officials urged Mainers to report unemployment fraud. By June 4, the state unemployment office sent an email to all claimants declaring the suspension of benefits until we could prove our identity. Validating my identity in response to the fraud submissions included two forms of a picture id and a selfie taken on the date of submission. To meet this requirement, I sent an email attaching a copy of my captain's license, passport, and selfie, confirmed by email on June 9. Benefits began again and were retroactive back to the date of the last suspension.

The boatyard went through a series of changes as it readied itself for the season on May 1 since they fell into the marina category defined in Stage 1 of Maine's reopening. The launch service became a primary focus to meet the COVID-19 checklist requirements. Six passengers were the maximum allowed on each launch, and a reservation system needed to be defined. As the boatyard webmaster, it was my job to locate a reservation system for three launches and a limited capacity. First, we divided the mooring field into red and green zones, with the demarcation line running from the dock to buoy number fifteen. Two launches would be dedicated to the green zone, while one went to red. I located a reservation system that I could customize to the three launches, each leaving the dock on staggered hours. Boatyard members reserved a launch date and time online when they wanted delivery to their boat. Only two passengers per family were allowed in any single reservation; beyond that, they waited at the dock for a pickup. A launch service page was added to the boatyard's website and went live on April 26. I was unsure how this would work with my business, given the launch limits and time constraints. Fortunately, on June 26, I no longer needed the reservation system. Guidelines for the launches changed, allowing the maximum capacity for each launch.

For any business to reopen, it had to commit to complying with the industry-specific checklist of requirements by filling out a short online form. Once completed, badges by the DECD became available to post on their doors, website, or social media channels to help instill consumer confidence in their operations. By June 26, the checklist for my business finally became available. I filled out the online form, followed by downloading the image, posted it on the website, and updated the information on my official July 1 reopening. I updated the availability calendar removing the "ON HOLD" message and set July 1 through October 5 as available. The season would be only fourteen weeks in length, and I was hoping for the best now that the doors were open. On July 1, I stopped submitting my weekly certification to the Department of Unemployment. I needed boat supplies for the season, and the marine store finally offered curbside pickup. Locating sanitizing wipes and hand sanitizer was a challenge, but perseverance won out. Since the boatyard restricted access to only members, I got the boatyard to allow me to mail a copy of my second parking pass with the date of their visit printed on it to my customer before arrival. Along with the usual information that I sent the customers, I included the summary of changes[37] for this season. The summary listed the restrictions for this year, a COVID-19 self-screen checklist, and the current quarantine guidelines, both state and federal.

For whatever reason, the season flushed out more folks who wanted to learn to sail rather than requesting a charter. The pandemic made people want to get outdoors in any capacity possible. By July, you could not find a bike, kayak, or canoe anywhere. Boat sales soared everywhere. People were desperate, all to my advantage. Bookings started flooding in as soon as my virtual doors opened. Many of my customers were staying in Maine from far off locations, working remotely. The boatyard required masking while on the premises and the launch, but once they were aboard the Marisa III, I made them optional since the risk was minimal. On a rare occasion, I gave a mask to a customer who had forgotten theirs as I carried several in a Ziploc bag within my carry-on. At the end of each outing, I would wipe down the boat with disinfectant wipes, sometimes with my customers' help.

I kept abreast of the ever-changing state guidelines throughout the summer season, hoping that charter boats or marinas would not have to shut down. By the end of July, our DHHS Commissioner said, "No additional states are being added to the exemption list. Currently, the states exempt from travel restrictions are New Hampshire, Connecticut, Vermont, New York, and New Jersey." All other states needed to either quarantine or show proof of a negative covid test within seventy-two hours of arriving in Maine. If ever there was a year to discover Maine and all of its glory, it was this summer as long as you were a Maine resident. The parks, seaports, restaurants, and other sites were pretty much free from tourists making many spots almost empty.

Given the late start to the season and the reduced number of bookings, my wife and I took advantage of the situation, exploring parts of our beautiful state that we had not seen before. I soon realized what I was missing having a sailing business during the best months in New England—having the time to take family members out for a sail, helping them relieve their stress, escaping the pandemic, and all of the depressing news. The more time I spent with my family, the more I felt an end to the business was not far off that this would become my final season. When the season opened, I set the last day during the first week of October, which was typical from years past. That changed when we learned our granddaughter, Marisa, was coming home for a week to surprise her mother for her birthday at the end of September. I could not miss this special occasion, and since I had no bookings from the twenty-second on, I backed up my closed days to that date.

In summary, for this unprecedented season, the number of lessons far exceeded the charters by a three to one margin. I attribute this to the reduced capacity to two. Through the summer, I would get a small family calling to go out for a charter, saying they were all related, thinking that my COVID-19 restriction didn't apply. I would tell them, "But I am not related." and direct them to other charter companies that would be willing to take them out. My season ended with thirty-five customers from eleven states, including California, North Carolina, Colorado, thirteen charters, and thirty lessons. Not bad, given the world situation and a much shorter season.

On the last day of the business, I met a news reporter from our local NBC affiliate for an interview. A week before, I submitted a story suggestion to the station regarding closing my business, briefly describing how long it has been in existence. It must have been enough for them to give me a call, seeking more information with the possibility of a human interest story for their newscast. I spent a little over twenty minutes with Hannah Dineen as she asked one question after another, and it was then she asked, "Could we meet at eleven-thirty next Monday the twenty-first to continue the interview?" My last day and my final customer scheduled for a late afternoon charter. I, of course, said yes. I then asked, "How will I recognize you?" to which she replied, "I will be the one with the camera gear."

I was at the dock by eleven on the twenty-first, waiting for Hannah and her camera person to arrive, and to my surprise, Hannah showed up alone with a large tripod and video camera bag ready to go. Knowing I had customers scheduled for a two o'clock sail, I asked how long might the interview take, and Hannah said, "About a half-hour should do it." I helped her load her equipment onto the launch and again when we arrived at the Marisa III. I wasn't sure how the interview would work, but I was overjoyed when she asked if we could take the boat out for a sail while she conducted the interview. The winds were light, the weather warm for late September, and no clouds in the sky. I cast off while she filmed my readying the boat. Once I cleared the anchorage, I fully opened the headsail and cut the engine. I took my usual position on the starboard cowl sailing over to Great Diamond. She grabbed her video camera and went below for some footage, then to the bow for more. While she was at the bow, I made a quick call to the boatyard restaurant to postpone my reservation to one o'clock; I saw I would not get back in time. She returned to the cockpit, set up the tripod, aimed the camera my way, and started the interview. At twelve-forty-five, Hannah noticed the time and was shocked how much time had passed. Sailing on Casco Bay will do that, so we headed back to the dock. Hannah had plenty for her story, and she was able to piece together an excellent rendition of my transition into my second retirement. It appeared on the nightly news that evening. The following is the result of her fine work.

Launching a new career in retirement
Author: Hannah Dineen (NEWS CENTER Maine)
Published: 6:55 PM EDT September 21, 2020
FALMOUTH, Maine — After decades of working in IT for various software companies, a Standish man decided to pursue his dream job as a sailboat captain.

Seventy-year-old Captain Lyman Stuart says, "You know you're in the right job when you get your paycheck and you think to yourself—and they pay me for this?!"

Ten years ago, Stuart began turning his passion into his profession. He got his captain's license and began using his vacation days from his IT job to take people out on the water.

"Shaking up your life every once and a while is a good thing,"

Stuart said. He believes his generation of baby boomers is redefining what retirement is, with many people considering it an opportunity for a career change.

Eventually, Stuart launched his own sailing company, Go Sailing Casco Bay, in which he takes private groups out for charter sails or sailing lessons. It's a company of one.

"I have no employees, no staff. It's just me... me and my boat," Stuart says.

It's on his boat that Stuart has shared his love of sailing with hundreds of people from across the country.

He says, "It fills my heart knowing I've helped other people discover what sailing is all about."

Part of that lesson is to teach them to live in the moment.

"Take time to slow down and enjoy the day... enjoy the ride while it's here."

On Monday, September 21, as he prepares to host a couple for a charter sail, it appears to be just like any other day, but it's not. It's the company's final day.

"Yeah, last customers are this afternoon and then we close it up!"

For Stuart, it's retirement act two.

"I feel like I've accomplished what I originally wanted to," Stuart said. He's looking forward to spending more summer days out on the water with his wife as opposed to customers.

That said, Stuart isn't exactly ready to sail off into the sunset just yet.

"I guess the next adventure after this is the book that I'm writing!"

The book is about how Stuart started his company and his transition into his "retirement career."

He hopes to be finished with it by next spring.

That next chapter will certainly be as fulfilling to him as his previous two. [38]

Knowing my afternoon customers were my last, I reflected on what I had accomplished over the past several years. I read somewhere that "Life begins at the edge of your comfort zone." So true. It was a common phrase I would share with passengers whenever they showed a little hesitation while underway. Sailing is a series of comfort zone edges as you expose yourself to varying conditions and situations. Through these, you become a more accomplished sailor. I hope that I helped many people become more accomplished in their pursuit of sailing and that now they are enjoying the same thrill that my father rooted in me so many years ago.

"Twenty years from now, you will be more disappointed by the things you didn't do than those you did. So throw off the bowlines. Sail away from safe harbor. Catch the wind in your sails. Explore. Dream. Discover."

- Mark Twain

PART 3

September 23, 2020: It has been a wonderful ten years, and I will cherish all the memories the hundreds of customers have given me. You were all special, and you are what kept me going out on the waters of Casco Bay. It was not an easy decision, but it was time to shake up my life and put it in a new direction. I hope every one of you will discover the thrill of sailing."

12 CLEANUP

The day after my last day, I began the process of closing down the business. It's not like turning off the lights and locking the door on the way out. As much effort as I had put into making my business visible to the internet, I now needed to make my business invisible and reduce the traffic to my website—a strange concept, but for the customer's sake, a necessary task.

My approach will start first with the low-hanging fruit. I will look at the business services no longer needed as the business will be closed. From there, I will branch out, locating websites that point to my website or business. It would make sense to work outside in and not make people believe that I am still open, frustrating folks in their efforts in finding a sailing school or charter. Closing down is going to take some time and a bit of research. I will need to locate all backlinks, a link from one website to another, in this case, links that point to my website.

I needed to update my website as my first task, stating that the business is closed and disable all the "Order Online" buttons within the Lessons and Charter pages to prevent folks from purchasing an event. I'll leave the contact information available just if they want to reach out to me with questions. They may be a prior customer. On the home page, I have a section titled "What We Do," which I will change to "What We Did." leaving the "Do" but with a strikeout through the word. The remainder of the site I will leave intact for now. I am sure my repeat customers will start visiting come springtime or during my annual February discount period.

As my business email will continue beyond the business closure, it didn't need the automatic insertion of my business signature, so I removed it from my email software and phone app.

Since the business is now closed, I no longer needed the commercial insurance on the boat. So I contacted my insurance agent to explain my situation. From her end, she emailed me the online cancelation form requiring a digital signature and date. An easy process and completed within a half-hour, then sent to the insurance carrier to finish the process. Given that the policy was effective until next May, I would receive a prorated refund for the unused premium. I now will add watercraft coverage through my homeowner and auto insurance carrier. As it turns out, my insurance agent found a better deal with another company, which included hurricane haul out and towing coverage allowing me to cancel two more stand-alone policies.

There are a few icon links on my website's home page; each needs addressing as they have backlinks into my site. The first of which is TripAdvisor. TripAdvisor does not allow removing a business listing but instead asks you to mark the business as permanently closed. According to TripAdvisor, *"We understand that some businesses might want to remove their listing for a variety of reasons. However, it is our mission to be a comprehensive source of travel information for our users. We only remove listings under specific circumstances."* I will try to get TripAdvisor to change the business profile reflecting a closed business while conforming to their guidelines. The change will take up to two business days for processing as their editors review it; all denied. They do not understand that my goal is to reduce traffic to my website, why not just delete the listing.

The remaining iconic links will change to their associated home pages once my specific listing no longer appears on their site.

I have a Facebook business page yet hardly ever used it. Just too much effort to continue posting new content. It was more of an experiment in social media, not to my liking. I don't have Instagram or Twitter accounts for the same reason. I don't see the need. The website was enough for drawing potential customers.

Given that, I still needed to remove the business page from Facebook and remove the link to my website from my personal Facebook account.

Google allowed me to mark my business listing as permanently closed, but for Google Analytics, I will keep it active. Google Analytics will be used to monitor my progress in hiding my website from the internet. Weird as it may seem, having zero activity on the website would be marked as an exceeds, but it will take work; it will be interesting to see how far and wide my business has spread on the world wide web. According to Google Analytics, I had forty-seven visitors in December 2020.

Yelp is similar to Google in that I can mark my business as permanently closed.

Bing does not offer the ability to mark a business as permanently closed like Google, so my only option was to delete the business listing altogether. For Bing analytics, I removed the site URL from Bing's webmaster tools and the file bingsiteauth.xml from the website.

Several services needed email requests to have my company unlisted on their website, requiring later verification of the completed task. These included Marine Waypoints, Visit Portland, EtravelMaine, Data Axle, and the Better Business Bureau, to name a few. I needed to obtain a new password for my listing on the Maine Tourism site since they changed their login service. Completing that, I found my listing and unpublished it.

My credit card processing company needed modifications to the online marketplace reflecting a closed business. I removed the items from the site, exported the customer list, item catalog, and the last two years of transactions to my computer for later referencing. In account settings, I selected the deactivate account option to finish the process.

A phone call was necessary to remove my listing from the online yellow pages. Calling the 800 number, I spoke to a customer service rep, who helped me through the process once I verified who I was. A next day verification proved that my listing and account no longer existed. The Dun and Bradstreet listing also took a phone call once I navigated through their lengthy phone menu system.

A few sites allowed me to delete my listing by logging into my account and perform the task online, which included deleting my account. Thumbtack and Brand Yourself are two examples. I wish more places offered self-management of your content.

My gosailingcascobay.com domain is coming up for renewal, so I decided to keep it for another year, changing the auto-renew option to manual and buying one more year. My thought is to continue showing my business as closed while folks continue to locate me through the internet. The ultimate hide is the dreaded "404 Not Found" page, but that won't happen until my domain finally expires.

A thought crossed my mind. Shutting down the business feels like I am a boy gathering the pieces of a toy that I have outgrown, wishing someone younger would enjoy it. Maybe. Possibly.

I would get regular emails from two monitoring services, which reminded me that they, too, needed addressing. One was Active Search Results, which improves a website's ranking in search results across several search engines. To be safe, I removed my website from the list of managed websites before deleting my membership. The other was Free Web Monitoring, which notifies me when my site is down and again when it is back up. Here, I deleted the reference to my website and then canceled my account.

Well, all of the easy stuff is complete, and I now need to do some digging to uncover those ancillary sites that I am not aware of and get those links removed. The research will require a useful SEO tool, several search engines since competing search engines use different methods to gather indexes, and Google analytics. I am sure this will be an internet fishing adventure, using search words and phrases as my lures. It should be fun.

I first needed to find the top, non-Google, search engines, and I found a list of seven; StartPage, Qwant, DuckDuckGo, Ecosia, Swisscows, Bing, and Yahoo. Some of these I have never heard of, so this should be amusing.

Starting with StartPage, I entered "Capt Lyman Stuart" in the search field and pressed enter. Never using this before, I found that it has a nice feature allowing me to visit any site in the results list anonymously. The first two results have already been taken care of, but the third, which I had forgotten about, did. I deleted the account to this site years ago, but the listing was still there. My recourse was to give them a call, yet I could only leave a message. I copied the URL to my listing, went to their contact page, filled out my request in the form provided, and pasted the URL into my description, and out it went.

Continuing through the results, I see I am listed in TripAdvisor of other countries, for I see I am on New Zealand's version; however, it's marked closed already.

Somehow my business ended up in Mapquest. Not sure how, because I do not remember adding it. At least it offered an easy way to mark the business as permanently closed. I received an email almost immediately stating that they created a ticket, and they will get to it "as soon as humanly possible."

I ended up as number six in a list of fifteen best things to do in Falmouth, Maine, on "the crazy tourist" website. Go figure. I never heard of this site either. Anyway, I sent my request to Jan via email, per her contact page. Await and see.

TripBuzz has me as number two with thirty-one votes and a ranking of ninety-seven percent. I was able to edit the listing through the "Suggest an Edit" option. It must have been an ancient listing as it still had the old website URL. After submitting the request, I received the following: "Thanks for suggesting an edit to this attraction. Our team will review your request and approve any edits to the listing as soon as possible."

Found out that there is a reference to my business on VRBO as a top attraction in the area. I spent a good fifteen minutes online chatting with one of their agents to see if there is a way to get my listing removed. It looks like they are drawing from Google Maps, and it made me revisit my business listing in Google, so I updated my business name by adding " - [CLOSED]" to the end of it. My thought is to have that appear in any listing when pulled from Google. VRBO is going to look at this on their end as well and let me know.

Still scanning down the list of search results revealed yet another unknown site that had a nice little writeup of my business, a travel site called "The Manual" showed a 2017 article "The Best Places to Play, Eat, and Stay in Portland, Maine." I sent a request via email to the editor in hopes I could have them remove it.

Changing my search within the same search engine to "gosailingcasco.com," I found a nail salon's Facebook page containing a website link to my website. I called the salon a got nowhere, so I emailed the business with a screenshot asking them to remove the link. Also found it on letsgotomaine.com's site and sent a removal request via their contact form.

Ok, enough for today. I will let those requests simmer for a while and check again on their progress before researching through the next set of search engines. I've added links to my browser, so it will be easier to revisit the sites already checked.

Three days later and I used the remaining six search engines, sending the same query into each. Although the results were different from StartPage, they were the same across all six and did not show anything new that needed addressing—mostly TripAdvisor reviews from my listing there.

Yext is a service I used initially to broadcast my business listing across a wide range of location-related directories from a single source. My business is now on twenty-one different directories, so I changed the information on the one form to reflect my closed business and let Yext publish the change to all twenty-one locations through a single save. I would encourage anyone with a company to utilize this free service to get your business on the many city directories worldwide from one source.

Another investigation tool is using a backlink checker for my domain. There are several, and many are free. Running my website URL through one only flushed out one more site that needed attention, and I had to send an email to request deletion of my business reference.

The last check is using Google's search engine to see where I rank in the results. I sent several criteria using many of the keywords I have seen others used to find me. I no longer appeared on the first page, which is what I was hoping from this exercise.

I will continue to monitor the progress as there are still some outstanding requests, and I'll keep an eye on my Google Analytics for weekly visitor counts.

The lights are off; the door is shut and locked. I put the key in my pocket.

13 FOR SALE

When I realized it was time to close the business during the final season, selling the business also crossed my mind. More as a curiosity than a reality. That curiosity grew from that same phone call by a person from Long Island, asking me how I ran my business. Would someone like to take over an existing, established business even if it was seasonal? It couldn't hurt to see.

In late August, I looked up business brokers in Portland to see how many there were. Quite a list. I chose a handful of brokers whom I felt could help me answer the question, is it possible. I left phone messages briefly describing what I was looking for to each, not knowing why none would pick up their phones. After a few days of no replies, I then sent emails describing in more detail what I would like to do along with a link to my website so they could see my business first hand—a few more days and again, no interest.

I was beginning to think this idea was going nowhere, and these brokers found no interest in selling such a small business.

I looked at the available brokers again and broadened my reach: more phone calls and more emails. I got the same results as the first round, so I put it to rest; however, it sat there in the back of my mind, stewing on its own.

The idea of selling resurfaced in early October during the business's closing when I thought of the outgrown toy analogy. At the same time, my wife had just completed a book club Zoom session and mentioned one group member in particular while explaining how their meeting went. She was a good friend of ours, and I recalled that she had sold her wedding planning business just before she and her husband moved back to the UK. She had not considered selling it until someone else told her to give it a try. "It couldn't hurt," the person said. I asked my wife to ask her who she used as the broker and email me their name. To my surprise, he was not one I had already contacted. I looked up his contact information and the company he worked for and gave him a call. No answer so I left a message, thinking it was going to be like the others. Imagine my delight when Michael Hall of the Jordie Lee Company in Portland returned my call the next day.

We had a great conversation, including a brief discussion about Diane, who emailed Michael's name. He said he would like to help me with the sale and asked me to send him four years of my Schedule C reports for his review and better understand my business. The next day, I emailed my profit and loss reports for the last four years, which are input into the Schedule Cs. I felt the details would give him a better view of the information since they showed a breakdown in terms familiar to my sailing business rather than the IRS report's generic terms.

Four days later, I received an email from Michael, thanking me for the information and telling me that he has arrived at a value. He had a high value and a low value, which included Marisa III. The draft listing agreement was attached to the email for my review. Within the agreement, Michael detailed our relationship's provisions, his commission when the business sold, and the retainer fee, which he would keep no matter what. After reviewing the agreement, I called him, and we scheduled a meeting at his Portland office in four days.

I arrived at Michael's office before he did, so I waited in the waiting area for him to arrive. The receptionist said he should be here shortly, and sure enough, Michael arrived on time. After greeting each other, we went into a nearby conference room. He asked if I wanted anything to drink, which I declined but thanked him for the offer. I was anxious to get started. He on one side, I on the other; we chatted for a bit before I asked him the questions that I had prepared. I knew the sale included the boat and the website domain; however, I let him know that my email address and phone number did not. Once I explained that these are still for personal use, he agreed. I also said that I would help the buyer with the website conversion and maintenance if they wanted to keep it for their purpose. Michael said that he had not sold a sailing business before but was intrigued at the opportunity to do so. I think he was looking forward to finding the right buyer, possibly a retired person with sailing experience living in Maine and having a sailing business on the side. Much like I did.

The rest of the time was mostly Michael asking me about my business, how it started, and my sailing background. We ended with each signing the listing agreement, and I wrote out the check for the retainer fee; copies were made and shared. Michael discussed the brochure development and what he would need from me to have one developed. The list included photos of the Marisa III, equipment on the boat, a maintenance list, and a 1974 Pearson review. I had my tasks, and Michael had his, as I departed the building and headed home.

I gathered the items for the brochure and uploaded them to a DropBox folder that I shared with Michael. Eight days after our meeting, the listing went up on their website.

To help promote the sale, I added a line to my website within my business closing message. A visitor randomly landing on my website may not have thought of buying a sailing business. Here was one ready to go. The line read, "I am now seeking a new owner to take over the business. If you are interested in this business, you can view the listing by clicking here." The ending was a link to my listing on the listing site offering an overview and a way to contact the selling broker, Michael.

A few days later, I received a draft of a most amazing nine-page brochure created by Deanna in the agency's marketing department. I only had a few changes to what they had, all minor adjustments, to which Michael said he would take care of. In his words, "I'm on it." The brochure was subtitled "Confidential - Offering Summary." Page two was an executive summary, followed on page three with the "About the Business." Page four was a collage of photos, then a list of equipment on page five. The remainder was the maintenance record, seller discretionary earnings, and area information for Portland and Cumberland County. I was impressed with how they utilized my pictures throughout the document. Only a serious potential buyer will get to see this wonderfully crafted selling tool.

My first listing report came to me via email from Michael in the middle of December. The report indicated that the ad was displayed fifty-seven hundred sixty times, clicked for details came to two hundred ten, and the number of times a buyer submitted a form (NDA) indicating interest in the business showed two. It is a beginning or an end, depending on how you look at it. The work is now in the hands of a professional doing the fishing for me, searching for that one potential buyer who would like to make sailing a business.

If the business does not sell, then I still have Marisa III. If it does sell, I will be looking for Marisa IV. I will continue to sail the coast of Maine and all of her bays for as long as possible.

* * *

FOOTNOTES

The following bracketed numbers are expanded references from within the book.

[1] American Sailing Association
[2] https://www.bplans.com/
[3] CG-719S
[4] https://www.mptusa.com/
[5] See Appendix
[6] Quicken Home and Business
[7] Offshore Risk Management Limited
[8] See Appendix [9] Microsoft OneDrive
[10] Microsoft's Expression Web 4.0
[11] See Appendix
[12] https://spark.adobe.com/
[13] See Appendix
[14] iPage.com
[15] Screaming Frog SEO Spider
[16] See Appendix [17] See Appendix
[18] See Apendix
[19] See Appendix
[20] See Appendix
[21] Pettit Hydrocoat Antifouling Bottom Paint
[22] Purogene water treatment
[23] Star Brite Sea Safe Boat Wash
[24] See Appendix
[25] Quicken Home & Business
[26] TurboTax
[27] Square

[28] availcalendar.com
[29] calendarpedia.com
[30] visitportland.com
[31] See Appendix
[32] See Appendix
[33] See Appendix
[34] See Appendix
[35] See Appendix
[36] See Appendix
[37] See Appendix
[38] To view the actual interview, see Appendix

APPENDIX

Throughout the book, I made several references to this section. I have created a website allowing you to view the specific examples as a reference for your use. The site is a single page and divided into sections. The Forms section has links to the two primary forms that I used in my business. The Miscellaneous section contains two of my promotional videos, a sample availability calendar, my home page as a pdf, and a copy of the contract I had with the boatyard. The other sections are chapter-specific as they represent and contain the reference material found in those chapters.

To view the reference material, enter the following in your browser: https://sites.google.com/view/referencematerial

Enjoy!

EPILOGUE

As of this writing, the business is still for sale, and there are a few outstanding items. In the spring of 2021, I will not renew my Maine LLC license ending my business with the state. I will print the final reports from my accounting software in preparation for this year's tax filing. After that, I will no longer need the software and its associated subscription fee; therefore, I will let it lapse. I will run the business sale process for one year, after which I will let it expire. My gosailingcascobay.com domain will stop in February of 2022. The final item is to cease the submission of a Schedule C within my tax filing in 2022. That is how the IRS will know that my business has ended. My business checking account will remain open and offer funds for my future sailing expenses.

ABOUT THE AUTHOR

Capt. Lyman Stuart

Lyman (Tadd) was born and raised in upstate New York; the Finger Lakes and Lake Ontario were his childhood playground and where his love for sailing began. It seems sailing was a Stuart trait, with father, grandfather, uncles, and cousins all took part in sailing throughout their lives. For the majority of Lyman's life, he worked in the  computer science field. In the early 2000s, he decided to live his passion. It is then he began to pursue his captain's license and formed his own sailing company. Now "retired" for the second time, he lives with his wife in Standish, Maine. He is a licensed captain, a certified sailing instructor, and holds a bachelor's degree in computer science from Franklin Pierce University. When he is not sailing on the waters of Casco Bay, he enjoys hiking, recording hikes for AllTrails.com, discovering new outdoor adventures, and reading.